Also by Will Wilkoff, M.D.

Coping with a Picky Eater

Is My Child Overtired?

The Sleep Solution for Raising Happier, Healthier Children

Will Wilkoff, M.D.

A Fireside Book
Published by Simon & Schuster
New York   London   Toronto   Sydney   Singapore

FIRESIDE
Rockefeller Center
1230 Avenue of the Americas
New York, NY 10020
Copyright © 2000 by William Wilkoff, M.D.
All rights reserved,
including the right of reproduction
in whole or in part in any form.

FIRESIDE and colophon are registered trademarks
of Simon & Schuster, Inc.

The chart on page 18 is from *Solve Your Child's Sleep Problems,* by Richard
Ferber, M.D. (New York: Simon & Schuster, 1986). Used by permission.

Designed by *O'Lanso Gabbidon*

Manufactured in the United States of America
1 3 5 7 9 10 8 6 4 2

Library of Congress Cataloging-in-Publication Data
Wilkoff, William G.
Is my child overtired? : the sleep solution for raising happier, healthier
children / Will Wilkoff.
p.   c.m.
Includes index.
1. Sleep disorders in children—Popular works. 2. Children—Sleep—
Popular works. 3. Infants—Sleep—Popular works.
4. Child rearing—Popular works. I. Title.
RJ506.S55 W55 2000
618.92'8498—dc21
00-041327
ISBN 0-684-86916-0

Acknowledgments

It doesn't take long for a pediatrician to realize that to succeed he must form partnerships with the parents of the children he is treating. Initially many of these partnerships were lopsided in my favor. In my first few years of practice I was often learning much more from the parents than I was teaching them. Eventually, I reached a state of equilibrium in which I was simply transferring what I had learned from some families to other less experienced parents. Of course I try to create an aura of professional mystique by putting my own spin on each lesson, but the truth is that I have become a middleman.

With this in mind, I must thank all of the parents of midcoast Maine who invited me to share in the care of their children. I will always be indebted to them for their trust and candor. They were eager to tell me when my suggestions worked and were kind enough to give me a second chance when they didn't.

On behalf of all of us who are concerned about children and their sleep problems, I would like to thank my medical school classmate Dr. Richard Ferber for sharing his research and his wisdom with us by writing *Solve Your Child's Sleep Problems*. The success of this classic work has begun to bring sleep deprivation the attention it deserves.

When I am speaking or writing on something that I feel strongly about, my passion can sometimes seduce me into climbing on the high horse that I keep tethered to the coat rack in my office. My wife, Marilyn, has cautioned me for many years to resist this temptation to pontificate, but Tricia Medved, my editor at Simon and Schuster, was more direct. With her number 2 pencil and an endless supply of pink Post-it notes, she worked for hours to eradicate the traces of orneriness from my tone. I must thank her for this and for her guidance when the project seemed to be lacking clear direction.

Finally, I would like to thank Jenn, Em, and Nick for putting up with a father who was either at the office or trying to embarrass them in front of their friends. Their ability to quickly adopt good sleep habits is just one of the many things that has made parenting them a joy for their mother and me.

W.W.

Brunswick, Maine

To Marilyn,
my wife and best friend

Contents

Introduction

The Wake-up Call

One afternoon a few years ago I was standing in the checkout line of our local supermarket waiting my turn when I overheard a discussion between two young women. The one whom I recognized was saying, "You know what Dr. Wilkoff would say? He would tell you to put him to bed earlier." The other woman replied, "I've heard his answer to every problem is to put your child to bed earlier." The first responded, "Well, for my kids that advice has worked almost every time I've tried it."

I knew it was going to happen sooner or later. I practice in a small college town on the coast of Maine, and word travels fast. Over the years I found that my advice often included recommendations about sleep; very often the message boiled down to suggesting that the parents get their child some more rest, and this usually included an earlier bedtime. Some doctors become fascinated with a narrow diagnostic category such as hypoglycemia or environmental allergy and try to explain every patient's problems in terms of their own professional obsession. Was it happening to me? Was I in a diagnostic rut? Was I telling parents to put their children to bed earlier just as a reflex?

That eavesdropping in the grocery store was a wake-up call, a reality check of sorts. For the next several weeks I started listening to myself as I navigated through my busy office schedule. I tried to be more objective. I tried to think of other causes for my little patients' problems, but sleep deprivation and fatigue continued to float to the top of my list of diagnoses and explanations. No, I wasn't going crazy; I had learned something valuable while practicing general pediatrics over the last twenty-five years. I was on the right track. I hadn't wandered out into left field. More than a quarter of a million patient encounters had taught me that sleep deprivation was a much more important health issue than it was given credit for. It was underdiagnosed and often mistreated.

With renewed confidence that fatigue really was the cause of many of my patients' problems this book was born. The doctor who was telling all of those concerned parents to put their children to bed earlier needed to write a book and explain that yes, sleep is critical to a healthy lifestyle. But it wasn't going to be as simple as just recommending earlier bedtimes. I would provide step-by-step instructions for weaving a variety of good sleep habits into the child-rearing process from birth to adolescence. I was confident that the same strategies I had been recommending to parents in Maine for the last twenty-five years would help other parents avoid the unfortunate fatigue-related situations I continue to see every day in my office.

What to Expect from *Is My Child Overtired?*

Tiredness Takes Its Toll

When I finally found the time to sit down to write the book, I set two goals for myself. The first was to convince as many parents as possible that fatigue is an important contributor to many of their child-rearing problems. You may already realize that sleep deprivation is nibbling away at your child's wellness, and see how it is eroding your happiness and effectiveness as a parent. Unfortunately, many parents fail to make the association between fatigue and their children's behavior problems. There are so many other things to blame: diet, hunger, illness, teething, anger, and boredom, to name just a few. But sleep deprivation should be at the top of the list.

Although you may understand that your child's crankiness is a message that he is overtired, there are scores of other fatigue-related symptoms you were probably attributing to other causes. The following list contains some of the conditions that are somehow related to sleep deprivation and that can be prevented by applying the sleep solution. I have included some obvious associations (such as crankiness) and some less-obvious ones (such as migraine headaches). This list is certainly not all-inclusive, but it does contain the symptoms and behaviors you are most likely to encounter as a parent. In a few instances sleep deprivation is the primary cause, and in others it is merely one of several contributors to the problem. Some of the conditions have a clearly demonstrable association with fatigue. However, some appear on the list because in more than twenty-five years of practicing general pediatrics I have observed that they are more likely to occur when a child is overtired. As I have reviewed the medical literature on sleep deprivation I have been pleasantly surprised that many of my clinical observations have been corroborated by research scientists.

A Partial List of Fatigue-Associated Conditions

Colic	Childhood migraine (including cyclic vomiting and abdominal pain)
Baby blues (postpartum depression)	
Divorce	Poor school performance
Accident-proneness	Child abuse
Auto accidents	Thumb sucking
Attention deficit disorders	Stuttering
Hyperactivity	Bed-wetting
Irritability and crankiness	Night terrors and nightmares
Depression	Sleepwalking
Tantrums	Nervous tics
Nocturnal leg pains (growing pains)	

A Blueprint for Raising a Well-Rested Child

My second goal is to supply parents with a collection of strategies that can help them minimize, if not eliminate, fatigue from their children's lives—and from their own lives as well. I will offer suggestions for organizing and reprioritizing your family's schedules and adjusting your parenting style to prevent sleep deprivation before it occurs. If your child already has poor sleep habits, you will learn how to improve them.

If you are a brand-new parent, you will learn why selecting the proper place for your baby to sleep is so important. Next I will walk you through the critical development of your infant's ability to put himself to sleep without your assistance. The acquisition of this skill of sleep independence is one of the cornerstones of raising a well-rested family.

As your child passes his first birthday you will be faced with the challenge of how to preserve his naps and still maintain an appropriate bedtime. You will learn the solution to this quandary as well as the answers to such frequently asked questions as: "When is the best time to move our toddler out of his crib and into a bed?"

With entry into kindergarten and grade school you and your child must juggle the demands of bus schedules, extracurricular activities, and homework into your lives and still leave enough time for rest and sleep. I can't tell you how to squeeze twenty-six hours of living into a twenty-four-hour day, but we will explore the most sensible and practical options for helping your child be alert and attentive in school and pleasant and well-behaved at home.

Unfortunately, your struggle against fatigue won't end with adolescence. In fact, most teenagers are sleep-deprived simply because their body's natural demand for more sleep is out of sync with the routines our society has established. Although you may not have much power to enforce your adolescent's sleeping patterns, you will learn about some strategies that may be effective. At least you will gain a better understanding of why your tired teenager behaves the way he does.

It's Never Too Late

Although prevention is an important component of the sleep solution, it is never too late to incorporate the basic principles of good sleep management into your child-rearing style. Don't feel overwhelmed or discouraged because your child is already five years old and you worry that you may have "done it all wrong."

In the beginning you may not have been very good about helping him learn sleep independence. He may still wander around with a blanket. His bedtime may be nine-thirty or ten, and yours is eleven. You may already have a poorly rested child, and in fact the whole family may be exhausted. You may have always known that he is overtired, and now you suspect that many of your child's most annoying behaviors and complaints are the result of sleep deprivation. The situation may seem hopeless and the problem too large to tackle. You probably don't even know where to start.

Don't get discouraged. We can fix it. Even if you haven't been successful at keeping yourself and your child well rested up to this point, there is a solution. I suggest you begin by reading the book front to back to help you understand the basic foundations of good sleep management. However, if you would prefer to dive right into the chapter that focuses on your child's age group that's fine, too. There are plenty of references to help you find related topics in the earlier chapters.

Although you may have missed the chance to prevent sleep deprivation when he was an infant, this is no time for guilt trips or pity parties. If you have a child between the ages of one and ten who desperately needs more rest, it is time to find a solution. Let's get on with it.

A Few Words About Gender

Because fatigue doesn't play favorites, I have chosen to refer to your child as "she" in half the chapters and "he" in the other half. In acknowledgment of the growing role of women in medicine, and pediatrics in particular, I have referred to all generic physicians as "she."

1

How Can I Tell If My Child Is Well Rested?

Step One: Suspect the Diagnosis

If your child is old enough to articulate her feelings, she may simply tell you that she is tired. However, most parents aren't this fortunate. Many five-year-olds with a thousand-word vocabulary will deny with their last waking breath that they need to go to bed, and then collapse into a deep sleep on the couch.

You may be able to tell when your child is tired by her behavior, but unfortunately many parents don't realize that their children are seriously fatigued. They may search for another explanation for a child's behavior when in reality sleep is the solution. Here are some ways to tell if your child is well-rested.

Let's Check the Numbers

Dr. Richard Ferber, clinical director of the Center for Pediatric Sleep Disorders at Children's Hospital in Boston, has kindly allowed me to reprint a chart from his classic book, *Solve Your Child's Sleep Problems* (Fireside Press). It clearly displays the relationship between age and sleep requirement.

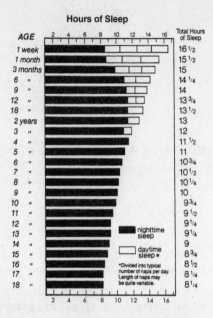

Hours of Sleep

AGE	nighttime / daytime sleep	Total Hours of Sleep
1 week		16 1/2
1 month		15 1/2
3 months		15
6 "		14 1/4
9 "		14
12 "		13 3/4
18 "		13 1/2
2 years		13
3 "		12
4 "		11 1/2
5 "		11
6 "		10 3/4
7 "		10 1/2
8 "		10 1/4
9 "		10
10 "		9 3/4
11 "		9 1/2
12 "		9 1/4
13 "		9 1/4
14 "		9
15 "		8 3/4
16 "		8 1/2
17 "		8 1/4
18 "		8 1/4

■ nighttime sleep
□ daytime sleep *

*Divided into typical number of naps per day. Length of naps may be quite variable.

FIGURE 1 Typical Sleep Requirements in Childhood

Like many other parents, you may be shocked to see how poorly your child's sleep patterns compare to Dr. Ferber's bar graph. You may be tempted to defend the situation by uttering the phrase I hear in my office on a daily basis: "My daughter [or son] just doesn't seem to need as much sleep as other children." You are probably wrong.

Yes, it is true that the sleep needs of individual children can vary widely, and Dr. Ferber's table should be used only as a rough guideline. However, in my experience most parents seriously underestimate their children's sleep needs. There are several reasons for this unfortunate miscalculation. One is the temptation to accept as normal certain fatigue-related phenomena such as falling asleep in the car or having to be awakened in the morning. Another is the failure of parents to recognize symptoms such as crankiness, temper tantrums, hyperactivity, headaches, and leg pains as manifestations of sleep deprivation. Instead these behaviors and complaints may be blamed on dietary deficiencies or some inherent personality flaw.

Carried by waves of technological change, our society has drifted from a lifestyle that was once dictated by sunrise and sunset. We have come to accept an abbreviated night's sleep as the norm. I continue to be troubled by how many parents believe that nine o'clock is an acceptable bedtime for a five-year-old who must be awake by seven to get ready for kindergarten. They wrongly assume that because their friends' children go to bed that late or later it must be normal.

There is a phenomenon scientists call "biologic variation." In simplest terms it means that we are all a little bit different. Your child may become tearful and clingy when she gets overtired. Mine may become belligerent and hyperactive. Your neighbor's six-year-old may appear to function perfectly well on ten hours of sleep each day, and your six-year-old may wake with fatigue-related leg pains if she gets anything less than twelve hours. It just happens.

I doubt that I will live long enough to see all of these differences and vulnerabilities explained, but I am sure that eventually scientists will be able to identify some of the minor variations in brain structure and chemistry that are to blame for these inequalities that at times seem terribly unfair. Don't wait for science to catch up with your own observations. Learn how *your* child's body and behavior respond to sleep deprivation and learn how much sleep *your* child needs. You can use Dr. Ferber's chart as a place to start, but your child's requirement may be slightly more than his table suggests is optimal. Don't compare your child's sleep patterns to her playmate's or her cousin's. You may be unaware of the problems their parents are experiencing. Each child has her own limits and peculiar ways of responding when those limits are exceeded. Yes, there are patterns, but treat your child as the special and unique individual that she is.

Here Are Some Clues That Your Child Is Sleep-Deprived:

Your Child May Not Be Getting Enough Sleep/Rest If . . .

- When compared to Dr. Ferber's table, her sleep deficit is more than an hour.

- She must be awakened in the morning.

- When allowed to sleep in the morning she sleeps more than a half hour longer.

- She falls asleep as soon as she begins an automobile ride.

- She is frequently cranky and whiny.

- She has numerous temper tantrums.

- It is hard to describe her as a happy child.

- She wants to carry a special stuffed toy or blanket all of the time.

- You frequently find her sucking her thumb.

- She often wakes at night with leg or foot pains.

- She frequently has what appear to be nightmares.

- She has severe afternoon or evening headaches that may be accompanied by vomiting.

- She seems distractible or hyperactive at times, usually in late morning or late afternoon.

- Despite doing well in grade school her grades begin to fall in middle or high school.

- She frequently says she is tired.

This is only a partial list. There are numerous other symptoms and behaviors that can be attributed to fatigue. If you can honestly describe your child as happy and content 95 percent of the time, your child is probably getting enough sleep and rest. However, if your child frequently seems unhappy or angry, and/or you aren't enjoying being a parent, it is time for the sleep solution.

2

THE SOLUTION CAN BEGIN BEFORE
YOUR BABY IS BORN

As a parent-to-be you must have been warned a hundred times
that your sleep patterns are in for a significant change. You have
already heard from your parents and friends with children that
when you finally "join the club" your baby will be waking frequently at night to be fed. With a smirk on his face your father
has reminded you about all of those hours he was up at night
walking the floor with you or about how he would have to take
you for a ride in that old Honda Civic to get you to sleep.

Sleep deprivation is just part of the package that comes with
new parenthood, isn't it? Sleepless nights are just the first install-
ment when you begin paying your dues, aren't they? Not exactly.
Of course, parenting a newborn is going to be tiring. His nutritional needs will demand that he be fed every few hours for the
first few weeks or months, but many of the horror stories you
have heard from exhausted parents were preventable. If you learn
a bit about the sleep patterns of babies and by organizing your
life and your home before the baby is born, many of the traditional problems with fatigue that you were warned to expect can
be avoided. This chapter will show you how, with a little thought
and planning, you can create an environment in which your
child can develop good sleep habits and you can keep sleep deprivation to a minimum. Although some of these recommendations are meant to be applied before the baby is born, don't fret if

you already have a baby. It isn't too late to get the ship back on course. Read on.

Where Will Your Baby Be Sleeping?

This may seem like a simple question, but the wrong answer can jeopardize your chances of success as you struggle with your first attempts at sleep management. The correct answer to "Where will your baby be sleeping" is "In his own room."

You may have assumed that the baby will sleep in your bedroom for a while and then move into his own room. The problem is defining what "a while" is going to mean. If this is your first child, I propose that two or three nights is the best answer, because I know that I won't get you to move him out sooner than that. A few experienced parents who have already learned a thing or two about sleep will have their newborn sleeping in his own room from the first night.

Why shouldn't your child be sleeping in your bedroom? For one thing, babies are noisy sleepers. They snort and sneeze. They rustle around. They breathe loudly and rapidly at times and then they will pause and seem not to breathe at all, certainly an unnerving experience if you are a parent trying to sleep just a few feet away.

"Sleeping like a baby" does not necessarily mean sleeping quietly. They are noisy little buggers and will unsettle the sleep of anyone trying to sleep in the same room. As a new parent you will need your sleep. We know that your sleep is going to be interrupted by your child's need to eat, but we don't want your sleep to be interrupted by those little noises that accompany his normal sleep patterns.

The other side of the coin is that your presence in the bedroom can serve as a distraction to the baby. Your noises may interfere with the baby's sleep. If your child has a premature wakening (often called an "arousal" and a normal part of the sleep cycle) and senses that you are in the same room, he may cry until you respond. If, however, your baby finds himself alone, he will resort to his own ingenuity to settle himself and go back to sleep. Don't worry about his being lonely. If you give him only half as much attention as I suspect you are going to lavish on him when he is awake, that will be more than enough to prevent him from feeling abandoned.

You may ask, "What about crib death? We're worried about not hearing our baby if he's in trouble." Although there has been one study that suggests that a baby sleeping in the same room as his mother may have a slightly decreased risk of crib death, this kind of survey has not been successfully repeated in the United States. The sad news is that your presence in the same room is not a guarantee of protection against the tragedy of crib death.

I have had patients die of crib death in their parents' bedrooms, even in their own beds. Crib death is a terrible tragedy, and we are still not much closer to an answer than we were twenty years ago, probably because there is no single answer.

> *As this book is being written, most pediatricians are instructing parents to put their children to bed on their backs to minimize the risk of crib death. Although there are a few dissenting voices, primarily those of older pediatricians, the "back to sleep" recommendation should be followed until more data is collected.*

When you become a mother, your hearing will seem to develop a special sensitivity that allows you to hear those important noises your baby will make—even though he may be in another room and you may have thought you were sleeping soundly. Barking coughs, the gurgles of a vomit about to happen, and the restlessness of a child with a fever are just a few of the sounds a mother can detect even though her child is one room away. Unfortunately, few fathers possess this special hearing acuity. It seems to be a peculiar sixth sense reserved for mothers, sort of an auditory maternal intuition. It penetrates doors and walls, ceilings and floors.

If it will make you more comfortable, purchase a monitor for daytime use. At night monitors can merely allow reentry into your bedroom of those nuisance baby noises I have warned you about. However, if your bedroom is on a different floor or level from your baby's nursery, a monitor is a good idea. It can also be useful if you have a large house or want to be out in the garden while your child is sleeping. But, if your child's bedroom is just a few steps away, I would discourage you from using a monitor at night.

What About Bed Sharing?

In the last few years an increasing number of parents have brought their newborns into bed with them. This trend toward co-sleeping has been fueled by a few reports that when infants and mothers sleep together their sleep cycles might change and synchronize. This observation has led some observers to theorize that bed-sharing may reduce the risk of sudden infant death syndrome (SIDS).

Babies who sleep with their mothers might feed more often, and if a baby is being breastfed these frequent awakenings and feedings might improve the chances of nursing success. In spite of these more frequent interruptions to feed some mothers have reported that they sleep better when they bed-share with their infant.

Although in some cultures bed-sharing is the norm, in North America this has not been the case. However, you may be tempted to create a "family bed" after your baby is born because it just sounds like the more natural way to raise your child. On the other hand, if the thought of sharing your bed with a three-year-old is troubling, you may have considered starting off by co-sleeping with your baby to take advantage of the safety and nutritional benefits you have heard about. Then when he is eight or nine months old, has passed the highest risk of SIDS, and is no longer relying on breast milk, you would plan to move him into his own crib.

Before you try either this shortened variation of co-sleeping or allow your child to share your bed until he decides to move into his own, let me offer you a few things to consider. First, bed-sharing has its risks. Babies have been inadvertently smothered by their parents or their parents' bedclothes. In fact, in 1999 the Federal Consumer Product Safety Commission warned parents against bringing children into their beds. They cited a study that found that over an eight-year period 515 children under age two (an average of sixty-four children per year) died as a result of sleeping in adult beds.

Second, the reduced risk of SIDS claimed for co-sleeping is controversial and not widely accepted. In 1997 the American Academy of Pediatrics' Task Force on Infant Positioning and SIDS stated: "There is no basis at this time for encouraging bed sharing as a strategy to reduce SIDS risk." It also warned that if a child is brought into bed, soft sleep surfaces should be avoided and "the bed sharer should not smoke or use substances such as alcohol or drugs" that may interfere with normal sleep patterns.

Although I believe that co-sleeping babies probably nurse more often and may experience better weight gain, there are numerous other strategies that can improve your chances for breast-feeding success that don't involve bed-sharing with your infant. I have watched thousands of babies who sleep independently gain weight very nicely on breast milk alone.

Although there may be some debate over whether co-sleeping offers any advantages, the majority of the parents in my practice who have tried it complain that they wake the next morning feeling tired as a result of their baby's frequent awakenings. However, the strongest argument against bed-sharing is that it can delay the development of sleep independence, which is one of the cornerstones of raising a well-rested child and the focus of the next chapter. If your child is going to form good sleep habits that include healthy bedtimes and adequate naps, he must first learn to put himself to sleep without your assistance. Co-sleeping will delay this process and can create sleep problems for you and your child. Unfortunately, waiting until your infant is eight or nine months old often makes matters worse because at that age he will be going through the normal stage of what is often called "separation anxiety or distress." It won't be easy to get him out of the bed that he has thought was his own for nearly a year.

What About Nursing in Bed?

Some mothers want to bring the baby into bed just for nursing. While occasionally this is fine, don't make a habit of it. Having listened to thousands of mothers describe their nursing experiences, I can tell you that at least half of the time when you nurse your baby in your own bed you and/or your baby will fall asleep.

Plan on doing most of your baby's night feedings in his bedroom. I realize that this means you must leave the warmth of your bed and walk on the cold floor to your baby's room. However, this arrangement will make it less likely that you will inadvertently co-sleep. As you are decorating the nursery, include a comfortable chair for yourself and a soft night-light at knee level or below.

What to Do If Your Baby Doesn't Have His Own Room

This situation can certainly present some problems, but often with some creativity there can be an acceptable solution. I can be very sympathetic to the plight of young married couples with small living quarters. My wife and I have been there and done that. Here are some suggestions that have been successful for my patients. I hope that they help you solve your bedroom deficiency.

First, take an inventory of all of the rooms, nooks, closets, and odd spaces that you have. I have known some families who have converted large closets into sleeping quarters for the baby. Remember, we are just looking for a place for the baby to sleep, we aren't planning a playroom or gymnasium. Some houses have an "extra" bathroom that with a carpet and some wall hangings can be made safe and quiet for an infant. That little den filled with boxes of books and unwanted wedding gifts could be made into a sleeping area. Rent one of those self-storage units that have popped up all over the country and put your extra "stuff" in it. It is probably much cheaper than moving to a bigger house or apartment.

The bedroom doesn't have to have a door, but it would be very nice if it did. If you rent, ask the landlord if you can hang a cheap door in the empty door frame. If this is really impossible (ask more than once) a thick drape or old bedspread hung over the doorway can keep the light out and the sound down. The room does not have to have a window, but it should be large enough to assure good ventilation. Install room-darkening shades or hang thick, opaque curtains.

If there isn't a room, partition off a corner of the living room with folding screens or heavy drapes or bedsheets. I realize this may raise havoc with your decorating scheme, but for now decorating isn't a priority. Move the TV, computer, and stereo equipment into your bedroom so that during the evening your baby can sleep with a minimum of visual and auditory interruption. So that you all can have your own space, consider temporarily converting your bedroom into the living room. Because the quantity and quality of your baby's sleep are so important, put your heads together and try to think of how you and the baby can each have a place for uninterrupted sleep.

Who Is Coming to Help You After the Baby Is Born?

This is really a ticklish question, but the correct answer can be important to your early success in family building. The first question could be, do you want an extra person around while you are trying to figure out how this parenting thing is going to work? Could you be asking for trouble? Is this a potential "too many cooks" situation? If there are two of you, there may not be much need for help in the first few days. With cooperation and close communication with your pediatrician, hospital, and visiting nurses the two of you can probably do a pretty darn good job of getting your new baby off to a good start.

Grandmothers can often provide some valuable assistance and have been the traditional first choice. Your mothers will probably be expecting to be called on. Even if their schedules make it difficult to come, they might be offended if you don't at least ask. However, if you would really like to fly solo for the first few weeks, don't be afraid to explain the situation: "Mom, we want you to come help if you can. Bob will be taking a week and a half off once the baby is born; it would be great if you could come sometime after he goes back to work."

Finally, what could be the most important question: Where will the "helper" sleep? Remember that it is imperative that the mother and baby get as much quality sleep as possible, and it is preferable for your baby to have a separate place to sleep. This is likely to mean that you just don't have a place in your home for the helper to sleep. I am troubled by the number of times I hear about a newborn's being pushed out of his own room and into his parents' bedroom to make room for his grandmother. Unfortunately, this kind of bed shuffling can result in a situation in which having a "helper" in the house actually makes it more difficult for new parents to get a good start. Of course, grandmothers don't intend to sabotage your early attempts at child-rearing. They want their grandchild to grow up healthy and happy, just as you do, but they may not realize how disruptive their presence in the house can be to your family's sleep needs.

How are you going to deal with this sensitive situation? You can use my name and refer your potential helpers to this book. You can tell them that you would love to have some help but that you've read that it is very important for the baby to sleep in his own room and you just don't have space for a guest to stay in your home. You would be glad to help them make reservations at a local motel or for them to stay with friends or neighbors. Reassure them that the new baby has generated a lot of extra work and you will appreciate their help with the cooking, cleaning, and laundry. You may find that some of the potential "helpers" suddenly develop schedule conflicts or bosses who won't let them take the time off.

I know that these last few paragraphs may sound like a condemnation of the extended family. There can be an important role for grandparents in those first trying months of parenthood, but they must realize that parenting (and grandparenting) is a gradual process of letting go. The new baby was yours to create and is yours to raise. Sure you will make some mistakes, but your parents need to respect your privacy and understand that your rest and your baby's sleep deserve a high priority. Your parents' efforts, as well-intentioned as they may be, should not be counterproductive. Coming to help you and then disrupting your usual sleep arrangements by displacing one or all of you from your beds just doesn't make sense.

Keep Things Simple

Plan now for the inevitable fatigue that you are going to face in the first weeks and maybe months of your parenthood by stripping your lives of any unnecessary frills and responsibilities. Your baby's life will be consumed by eating and sleeping. He should be learning to settle into your home schedule and developing good sleep habits. Try to trim your life and his down to the basics of eating and sleeping.

Don't plan any trips for the first few months after your delivery. Your infant shouldn't be doing any unnecessary traveling because traveling will probably disrupt his sleep patterns.

Prepare Yourselves for Too Many Visitors

I can promise you that your new baby will draw a crowd and with it overstimulation and fatigue. Try to balance your natural instinct to show off your baby with the reality that too many visitors can be exhausting. Friends and relatives who understand small children and who remember what it was like to be a new parent will usually call before they come over, and will first ask if there is something they can do, like shopping. They may simply drop off a casserole with a note that says "Reheat at 350 degrees for 20 minutes" and slip away without even ringing the bell. Although they may be eager to see your baby, they won't expect you to interrupt the baby's sleep merely so they can look at him.

They realize that the baby's sleep and your rest are far more important than their desire to see the baby. They know that there will be plenty of time for that later on. When visitors do stop by, don't be afraid to tell them when you are getting tired or need to leave the room to nurse your baby.

Make sure your answering machine is in good working order and turn off the ringer on the phone. You can update the message every couple of hours with fresh information about the new baby: "Jason is feeding well. He has peed six times today and has already had two wonderful mustard-colored poops. He and his mother are taking a nap right now. We will try to call you later."

> *Remember these courtesies you are learning when it is your time to be the friend of a family with a newborn.*

Plan to Work as a Team

Dad can take over many of the tasks that have traditionally been Mom's responsibilities. This may mean shopping, doing the laundry, or planning and preparing the meals. If you have already had a less-traditional division of labor, there are still going to be gaps for a husband to fill when his wife has made that transition into motherhood. While Dad can't breast-feed the baby, it is important for him to create a positive attitude about the nursing and do as many of the other baby maintenance things (such as diaper changes and bathing) as he can to allow Mom to get her rest.

Purge Your Appointment Book

Look at your social and work schedules before the baby is born and trim away the unnecessary obligations for the first couple of months after the baby is home. Like most parents, you will underestimate the amount of work that having a new baby entails and may fail to make adequate adjustments in your schedule to minimize the inevitable fatigue. By having a child your life has changed forever. Priorities are going to have to change. If you agreed to be a bridesmaid for one of your college roommates and her wedding falls in the first few months after your delivery, you are going to have to make some hard decisions. You may have to cancel out, or only attend in a limited fashion. The annual reunion of your championship high school football team that you have never missed may have to go on without you this year. There is life after children, but it will take you a while to rearrange priorities and get your baby settled in and sleeping well before you can resume a schedule that bears any resemblance to your former life.

Plan on Taking Your Full Maternity Leave

Arrange for a few more weeks if possible. If you are planning to breastfeed, you should realize that the longer you can stay at home, the more likely it is that you will succeed in combining nursing and your job. I view a two-month maternity leave as a minimum. You will need at least that long to recover from the fatigue of pregnancy and the frequent feeding pattern of the first few weeks. Three months is significantly better and four months would be great. Be very cautious about agreeing to return to your job early "for just a few hours each week" to help out. These deals always seem to expand into more than you bargained for. I know that many employers take a very hard line about maternity leave, but it never hurts to ask, beg, and negotiate with your boss. Don't be afraid to request a supporting letter from your pediatrician.

• • •

You have already thought about some of these issues, but I suspect you have seriously underestimated how tired you will be during those first few months. Now is the time to begin to rearrange your priorities. Keep your rest and your baby's sleep high on the list. It will make your transition into parenthood so much easier.

Summary of Strategies

- Provide a separate sleeping space for the baby, preferably with a door. Be inventive if a room doesn't exist.

- Plan on having the baby sleep in his own room/space after you have been home for three or four nights.

- Promise yourself that the baby will not sleep in your bed.

- If you are going to have a "helper," make sure that she won't be displacing you or your baby from your beds.

- Define for the "helper" what you expect she will be doing.

- Strip your life down to the bare essentials. Parenting is going to take much more time and energy than you think it will.

- Don't plan on taking long trips or attending weddings or family reunions for the first few months after the baby is born.

- Take the full maternity leave that you are offered. You will need it.

- Plan to work as a team so that you can all stay as rested as possible.

- Move your baby's sleep schedule and your rest to the top of your priority list.

3

The First Six Weeks

The First Milestone: Healthy Weight Gain

Before you can begin guiding your baby toward healthy sleep habits, you must be sure that she is healthy and gaining weight. As I hope your pediatrician has warned you, all babies, both breast-fed and bottle fed, will lose weight over the first week or so. This loss can be as much as 10 percent of their birth weight, meaning that a ten-pound baby might drop as much as a pound.

Steady weight gain after this initial loss is the *first milestone*. It could take only a week or as long as a month. Schedule a visit with your pediatrician to have your baby weighed during the week after you go home from the hospital. You will feel much better knowing that your baby is starting to gain. That first trip to the doctor may provide ample reassurance that your child is on a good nutritional path, or it may take as many as half a dozen visits. Unfortunately, if you are nursing your baby, you can't measure your milk output by watching the level in a bottle go down. You may not be able to pump out much milk, but that doesn't necessarily mean your baby isn't being satisfied. Like most mothers, you will worry that your baby isn't getting enough to eat. Do whatever it takes to convince yourself that your baby is drinking enough to grow at a healthy rate. We can't even begin to talk about sleep until she has reached that milestone.

If the pediatrician you have selected doesn't seem eager to see your baby for a weight-check appointment during that first week, be assertive and ask (demand, if you must) that she see your baby so that you can be reassured. Don't be afraid to ask for more follow-up weight checks until *you* are convinced that your baby is healthy and gaining weight well. If you sense resistance from the pediatrician, it may be time to find another doctor. Don't read any farther until you have reached this first milestone. It will be impossible to follow the recommendations contained in the rest of the chapter until you and your pediatrician are comfortable with your baby's health and nutrition.

If your baby has not begun to gain adequately, you and your pediatrician can begin to find a solution before the problem becomes too complicated. The answer may be as simple as waiting a few more days for your milk supply to become more established. Particularly if you had a long labor or a difficult delivery, it may take a week or two for your milk to come in fully. You could be anemic or have an infection that may be limiting your body's milk-producing capabilities. Check with your obstetrician to make sure you are healthy.

Sometimes feeding schedules must be developed. You may be feeding too infrequently or too often, too long or not long enough. Contact a lactation consultant, particularly if you and your baby are having trouble coordinating the mouth-to-nipple connection.

Your baby may not be gaining because she is sick. Your pediatrician will be alert to this possibility and should examine your child carefully. She may order some blood and urine tests if she suspects an infection. We can't think about sleep issues until your baby is healthy and gaining weight consistently. Usually those three things go hand-in-hand-in-hand.

The Second Milestone—Mastering Sleep Independence

Once your child is gaining weight consistently she is ready to *learn how to put herself to sleep in her own bed in her own room.* Helping your child develop sleep independence is really the first step in the twenty-year process of gradually transforming your child from a fetus who was totally dependent on its mother to an adult who can support herself in society. By the time your baby is four years old she will have learned to walk, talk, feed, and dress herself. Eventually she will have developed the skills to obtain her own food and shelter and live on her own. Raising her will be a long, slow, and sometimes painful process of letting go. The first step in this transition is accepting the fact that falling asleep is not something you can do for your child. Your role is merely to create a situation in which she can quickly learn to do it herself.

Some pediatricians and sleep experts might advise you to wait until your child is between four and six months old before beginning to encourage sleep independence. Unfortunately, there are hundreds of thousands of parents who have endured months of sleep deprivation unnecessarily because they had been led to believe that their babies were too young to learn good sleep habits. To make matters worse, with every passing week their babies are forming more bad sleep habits and associations that will be difficult to undo when they are older.

In more than twenty-five years of pediatric practice I have found that most babies will respond to some gentle tinkering with their sleep schedules well before the commonly cited six-month guideline. In fact, a few babies are ready to learn to put themselves to sleep as early as two weeks of age, and almost all are ready before they are one month old. Once your baby is gaining weight consistently you can begin to look for ways to get yourself a bit more consistent sleep. Of course you are going to get up several times at night to feed your baby, but there are things you can do to make sure all of these awakenings are really necessary. The suggestions about setting up your home and the child's bedroom that you found in the last chapter are essential for success.

The rest of this chapter will provide step-by-step instructions for developing and implementing a strategy that will allow your child to develop sleep independence, the *second milestone.*

First, you must adopt the attitude that it is *not* your job as parents to get your child asleep and then put her to bed. It *is* your responsibility to create a safe and comfortable bedroom and to assure that your baby is healthy and well nourished. This means that whenever possible you should be putting her in her crib awake. Of course, this isn't always possible because she will occasionally fall asleep while she is feeding. This is particularly true at night and in the first few weeks after birth when babies often seem to spend most of their time sleeping. Later in this chapter I will explain how to safely limit your baby's feedings so they won't interfere with your efforts to help her attain sleep independence.

Raising a well-rested child will often mean stepping back to see whether your parenting techniques are reinforcing good or bad associations. For example, if you allow your child to fall asleep while she is feeding, she will probably expect to be fed whenever she is sleepy. As she gets older she may wake at night even when she is not particularly hungry. And if she has come to expect that a feeding always precedes falling asleep, she is going cry until you feed her—not because she is hungry but because for her sucking on a bottle or at your breast has become associated with the process of going to asleep.

You may find it difficult to accept the notion that you should be putting your baby in her crib while she is awake. Your parents may be even more surprised by this advice because they always rocked you or walked the floor with you until you fell asleep. As the well-rested parent of a well-rested child, you won't be pacing the floor or taking your baby for a ride in the car at two in the morning because that is the only way she will fall asleep. Your baby can and will learn how to put herself to sleep in her own crib.

The concept of putting your baby to bed awake may strike you as unnatural. However, just think about it for a moment. You don't fall asleep on the couch and expect your spouse to drag you into bed. When did you learn how to fall asleep in your own bed? How old should your child be before she learns that same skill? The advocates of co-sleeping might answer that the child will tell you when she is ready. However, once you are sure that your baby is gaining weight and the pediatrician tells you she is healthy, it is time to start the process. Your role is merely to create a situation in which she can quickly learn to put herself to sleep. The rest of this chapter will show you how to do it.

How to Help Your Baby Achieve Sleep Independence

First, Understand That Your Infant Should Be Sleeping Most of the Time

In the first few months of life your child really has little else to do except sleep and eat. Look back at Dr. Ferber's chart on page 00 in chapter 1. Notice that your new baby should be sleeping fourteen to sixteen hours per day. In the first month your child may be feeding as many as eight to ten times per day. If each of these feedings takes half an hour (and, trust me, in the beginning you both will be much less efficient than this), that doesn't leave a whole lot of time for anything else. Extended activity is likely to overstimulate your baby and interfere with her sleep cycle. Babies in the first four to six weeks of life really don't require much stimulation and interaction. They don't get bored, and it is certainly not your job to keep your baby entertained. If she seems bored or fussy she probably is just tired.

Although you would like to believe that your child has great capacity and need for play with you, she really doesn't, at least during these early weeks. During the day her playtime should be limited to just fifteen or twenty minutes after a feeding. If she gets cranky or falls asleep before this time you should be putting her down even sooner. The more tired you allow her to become the more difficult it will be for her to fall asleep and the more likely it is that she will wake sooner.

I know that doesn't make sense, but that is often the way it works. As time passes the number of feedings and the time per feeding decrease. Your child's need for sleep still remains quite high, but the time once spent on feedings will become playtime. The pie graphs give you a feeling for how this will change over time.

one-month-old

one-year-old

Keep Feedings Short

An important factor in the success of your child's reaching the second milestone is the length of her feedings. If a feeding takes too long your child will fall asleep during the feeding and not in her bed as we hoped. She will begin to associate feeding with sleeping, and you will be locked into the situation where you have to feed your child for her to sleep.

> *Remember, you are feeding your child so that she will grow, not so that she will sleep.*

This statement may be shocking to you, and it will surely run counter to some of the advice you will receive from parents and friends. But think about it. Although your child may not want to sleep if she is hungry, sleeping and eating are separate bodily functions and should be kept that way.

If the feedings are too long your child may become overtired, and as I have warned you, fatigue can interfere with her sleep patterns. Lengthy feedings may contribute to premature wakenings and shortened sleep cycles. Whether your child is nursed or bottle-fed, a feeding doesn't really need to last more than twenty minutes—half an hour at most. If your baby is bottle-fed she should be able to get as much formula as she needs in twenty minutes as long as the nipple is flowing adequately. Make sure that the nipple holes are large enough so that when the bottle is tipped upside down it will steadily *drip-drip-drip-drip*. Ask your pediatrician or an experienced parent if he or she thinks the nipples you are using are adequate. If you allow bottle feedings to straggle along for forty-five minutes or an hour it will be difficult, if not impossible, to establish a healthy sleep pattern.

> *If your child was premature or has some medical problems, consult your pediatrician before following any of these suggestions about feeding times.*

If you are breastfeeding, most of your milk is pumped out in the first five to seven minutes per side. There is usually no reason for a nursing to last more than fifteen minutes on each side. If you are worried that this time limit is too short, go to the pediatrician and ask her if your baby is growing adequately. If you allow a breastfeeding session to last longer than thirty minutes in total you run the risk of becoming a pacifier for your baby. Remember, we don't want your baby to fall asleep while she is feeding, whether it be at your breast or with a bottle.

During the first few weeks you will be inefficient no matter how you feed your baby. You will forget the spit-up cloth. You will have misdiapered her and she will poop all over you midway through the feeding. If you both need a change of clothes, that will make the feeding take even longer. As days go on you will gain efficiencies as both you and the baby learn the ropes.

Set a Day-Night Pattern

It will be easier to help your child develop sleep independence if you begin by creating a distinct day-night pattern. You may have been warned that babies often have their days and nights mixed up. I suspect that at least 75 percent of the families I have worked with have experienced this frustrating flip-flop. During the first few weeks of life most babies seem to prefer to be more active at night and sleep longer stretches in the day. The difficulty comes when *you* allow your own day-night cycle to become reversed. Some parents abandon their familiar awake/day–sleep/night pattern and follow the bizarre (but normal) sleep patterns of a new infant who is just a few days old. Don't let yourself fall into this trap.

Of course, you are going to have to get up at night to feed and change your baby, but this doesn't mean that you need to begin doing laundry, reading books, watching TV, or playing kootchie-koo from midnight to four in the morning. To be successful in sleep management you must resist turning your night into day just because that is your baby's preference. Remember, you can't afford to take several naps during the day the way your baby can. You must assume a leadership role on this issue. Make it clear to your baby by your actions that while you will get up at night to feed and change her you are not going to stay up and play.

To help your baby ease into a more humane day-night cycle, I suggest that from 7 at night (it could be 6:30 or even 8 if you wish) until 7 in the morning you leave your baby in her bedroom with the shades drawn and the lights out. Use a small night-light located at or below knee level. Of course, you must still respond to your baby's cries for food. However, feed her and do her diaper changes in her darkened room. Your eyes will easily adjust to the dark. Don't worry; you won't put the diaper on the wrong end.

After the feeding and changing resist the temptation for an active interaction and then promptly put the baby back in her crib. Your goal is to demonstrate to your baby by your businesslike manner that nighttime is for sleeping and feeding only, not for playing.

During the day—that is, from 7 in the morning until 7 at night—your baby should continue to sleep in her crib, in her bedroom with the room-darkening shades drawn. However, when she awakens to eat, take her into the living area for the feeding. In this more stimulating environment your child will hear the usual household noises, smell the interesting kitchen smells, and see the bright colors and movement associated with other family members.

After these daytime feedings take the opportunity to play with your baby if she is alert and interested. When she seems to be losing interest return her to her darkened bedroom while she is still awake. Remember, in the first month or two this playtime really doesn't need to be, nor should it be, much more than fifteen or twenty minutes. Feeding, particularly breastfeeding, provides most of the positive parental interaction for these very young infants. Most of the playing in these first few weeks is more for your amusement than your child's benefit.

I am not suggesting that you should try to keep your child awake during the day so that she will sleep better at night. That strategy almost never works—in fact, it usually makes things worse by overstimulating and exhausting your child to the point where she will have trouble settling down and going to sleep. Learn and accept this paradoxical relationship between fatigue and sleep now while your baby is just a few days old. It will make raising a well-rested child much, much easier.

> *If you allow your child to become overstimulated and overtired, she will have more trouble falling asleep and will be more likely to wake frequently once she falls asleep.*

If you aren't trying to tire out your baby, why even bother with this dark/light–night/day charade? The answer is that you want to demonstrate to your child by your actions and the atmosphere you create that you expect only certain behaviors at night, namely sleeping and eating. During the daytime your baby will have the opportunity for a broader range of behaviors that includes playing, observing, and being stimulated by her surroundings.

Establish a Healthy Bedtime

Start with a healthy bedtime and make lights-out at 7 or 7:30. One of the cornerstones of raising a well-rested child is the establishment of good sleep habits, and the first month is not too early to start. I know that 7 or 7:30 may seem early and a bit arbitrary, but let me explain why it isn't.

First, by starting off with an early bedtime when she is a newborn you will avoid the predictable and ugly struggle that will occur when she is three and you tell her that nine o'clock is too late. Habits and traditions that have become part of her bedtime ritual will be hard to break. An important principle of the sleep solution is putting your child to bed at a healthy hour, and for children under the age of six or seven this means 7 or 7:30. Instead of having to retreat as your child gets older, begin with an appropriately early bedtime from the very beginning.

Second, by establishing lights-out at an early hour, you will leave yourselves a few hours to relax and enjoy each other's company. Your marriage and your success as parents require that you both be well rested. If you have allowed your baby's bedtime to become 9:30 or 10, you won't be leaving enough time for this critical rejuvenation, or you will be going to bed so late that you will start the next day too tired to function cheerfully or effectively.

It is tempting to delay your baby's evening bedtime until it is nearer to your own. Just holding your baby and talking to her is fun. The novelty of being a new parent may seduce you into creating a routine that will be difficult to undo later. In the first few weeks your baby may be feeding so frequently in the evening that there seems little point in making lights-out as early as 7 or 7:30. Remember that extended activity past her healthy bedtime is likely to overstimulate your baby and interfere with her sleep cycles. During the first six weeks your baby doesn't require as much stimulation and interaction as you may think. She won't get bored, and it is certainly not your job to keep her entertained whether it is nine o'clock at night or two o'clock in the afternoon. If she seems bored or fussy she probably is just tired and it is time for her to go to bed.

Keep It Simple

The first few weeks with your newborn will be tiring and can be frustrating and confusing. If you are going to succeed in raising this little bundle into a well-rested child, you must simplify her life and yours. During her first year your baby doesn't have a job, and she doesn't go to school. She eats, she sleeps, and she plays.

A Place for Everything

To keep things simple, let's assign each of the baby's three activities to one location. First, whether she is bottle-fed or breastfed, she will feed in your arms in a cradled position. Second, when she plays she should be lying on your lap or in your arms in a face-to-face position. In the first few months of life "play" is going to consist of little more than talking, some tickling, and some bouncing. This is pretty basic stuff that can all be done in that lap position. The third activity, or inactivity in this case, is sleeping, and that should be done only in her crib. Of course, as your child gets older life becomes more complex and she will feed in a high chair as well as in Mom's arms. She will play on the floor as well as in her parents' laps. But she will always be sleeping primarily in her bed. Young children love consistency and routine; it may seem boring to you in the beginning but this simplicity of place and activity will pay big dividends in the short *and* long run.

To review, the three activities and their three places are:

Eat: Arms   Play: Lap   Sleep: Crib

Sounds pretty simple, and it is. Let's look at some of the problems you can get into if you stray from this arrangement. If you allow your baby to fall asleep while she is feeding in your arms she will begin to associate feeding with sleeping, and when you try to put her in her crib to sleep she will protest. If she awakens in her crib later on and just wants to go back to sleep, she will expect you to pick her up, cradle her in your arms, and probably feed her, even though she may not be hungry.

If your baby falls asleep in your bed while she is nursing, she will begin to associate your bed with sleep and not her own crib. Giving your baby a bottle in her crib is not only dangerous and bad for her teeth but can create a potentially unhealthy association between eating and sleeping.

Finally, what could happen if you encourage your child to play in her crib? First, if you are the one playing with her, you will probably overstimulate her, and she will have trouble settling down to fall asleep. Second, by encouraging play in her crib you are creating another set of confusing associations. If you accessorize your baby's crib with all sorts of gyms and toys she won't be sure when you put her down whether she is supposed to be playing or sleeping. Remember, we want to keep her life simple. When she is in her crib we want her to be sleeping. As she gets older she may naturally play with her own hands and talk to herself when she wakes in her own crib. That's just fine. Don't interrupt the natural development of that self-amusement skill. However, make it very clear by your behavior at bedtime, and by the things you put on and in her crib, that her bed is a place to sleep, not to play.

Don't Use a Swing!

Probably the best example I can think of to show the chaos that can occur when an activity is allowed to take place in an inappropriate place involves the swing. How are those unfortunate pieces of baby furniture supposed to be used? If they are for play, then they are a poor choice, particularly for babies less than three or four months old. It will be much more fun for you and certainly more beneficial for your child if her play involves direct physical contact with you. Playful and comforting touching is an important way for you to communicate with your infant who is too young to understand the words you are saying. In the first two or three months your child should be awake for only brief periods of time after a feeding. Take advantage of these little snatches of time for physical contact.

If you intend to use a swing as a place for your baby to fall asleep, then it will be creating a bad association. Remember, we want your baby to form a strong link between sleeping and her crib, and to make this easier she should have only one place to sleep. If you allow her to sleep in a swing she may begin to prefer it to her crib, and you will have a devil of a time getting her to accept her crib. You might be tempted to use the gentle rocking motion of the swing to help her fall asleep, and then transfer her to her crib. This isn't a good idea because she will either wake as soon as you move her or, if she wakes in her crib, you will have to return her to the swing so that she can fall back to sleep. A swing is inefficient as a sleep aid, and your baby will rapidly outgrow it in just a few months. More important, using a swing merely delays your child's attainment of that second milestone of *putting herself to sleep in her own bed*. To keep things simple, don't buy a swing. If you have been given one, you can use it as a play place as your baby gets old enough to enjoy a variety of activities (five or six months), but don't allow her to use it as a place to snooze. Car seats and rocking chairs can also cause confusion if you allow them to be used as places to fall asleep.

Don't Misuse a Snugli

Another piece of baby paraphernalia that deserves comment in this regard is the Snugli (one of those over-the-shoulder-carry-in-front-of-you baby knapsacks). Using a Snugli as a handy way to carry your baby when you go out for a walk is fine, but it can sabotage our attempts to help your child learn sleep independence. Lulled by the gentle motion and warmth of your body, your baby will probably fall asleep as you carry her. Although this may not be too much of a problem after she has mastered the skill of putting herself to sleep in her crib, it can of course confuse things at a stage when we are trying to simplify her life and develop good sleep habits and associations.

Some specialists in child behavior will advise you to use a Snugli as a way to calm your baby and get her some sleep while you are trying to get things done. A few of these experts might argue that carrying your baby around with you all day long is a more natural way to raise your child. I certainly agree that carrying your child around with you all day long can have its advantages, and it works for other cultures. The problem is that our society has evolved to a point that carrying your baby on your back or chest is impractical. For example, driving an automobile or sitting at a computer terminal with your child in a Snugli is either unsafe or difficult. For better or worse, our lifestyles require our babies to learn sleep independence that is not compatible with continuous maternal contact. In other words, if you are going to use a child carrier to make life easy for you, make sure your child has already reached the second milestone. Otherwise you run the risk of creating chaos by giving your baby one more confusing option when she is trying to decide where to sleep. Don't let a Snugli become just another place to sleep until your child has adopted her crib as her first and favorite choice.

Bassinet, Cradle, or Crib?

Most newborns don't like the wide-open spaces of a full-sized crib and will squirm and inch their way into a corner in an attempt to make their sleeping area feel more cozy. You can assist your baby in her efforts by creating a little nest in one corner with tightly rolled up blankets. Be careful to avoid loose pillows and other soft objects that could pose a risk for smothering.

Because of their smaller dimensions, bassinets and cradles have traditionally been first places for many babies to sleep. While in theory you might expect the transition to the unfamiliar surrounds of a crib to be difficult, it does not seem to happen very often. This is probably true because most babies develop an attachment to their blankets. By making sure that your baby's blanket moves with her when she outgrows the bassinet, you will keep relocation problems to a minimum.

About Burping

One of the big snags in helping your child develop good sleep habits can be burping. Many parents waste a lot of their waking time and their babies' sleeping time by overburping. Be assured that your baby will not explode if she hasn't burped. There is an opening at the other end of the system, and a good fart can be just as good as a good burp. Granted, your baby may have some abdominal discomfort or gas pains if she doesn't burp well, but keeping the child up for an extra half hour is usually not the solution.

Your child is responsible for burping herself. It is not something you can do for her. You can be a helper or an enabler, but burping is like falling asleep. You can create the proper conditions, but the final responsibility rests with your child. If your child is too tired or asleep, she won't burp as well as when she is alert. For this reason you should burp your baby early in the feeding (after one and a half or two ounces or mid-side if you are nursing). If she is still awake, she can be an active participant in the process. In addition, if you wait too long the swallowed air will have passed out of the stomach and into her intestines and is irretrievable by burping, destined to be heard later as a fart.

On the other hand, sometimes early burping is bad advice, because your baby may take offense at the interruption and cry harder and swallow more air. You will just have to experiment. The most important point is that you shouldn't be spending more than two or three minutes per attempt trying to get those burps up. The gas won't kill your child, and very often the discomfort blamed on gas is really just fatigue or at least is aggravated by fatigue. We will discuss this interaction of gas and fatigue in detail in the chapter that covers colic (see page 62).

Avoid Overstimulation

If your child is going to settle in and learn to put herself to sleep, you must be careful to keep her environment relaxing and peaceful. I have warned you that a child who is being overstimulated will have more trouble getting to sleep than a child who finds herself in a mellow atmosphere. Children come into the world with varying abilities to tolerate chaos. Some babies are so laid-back that they can fall asleep in a shopping cart at the grocery store. On the other hand, your child may be so high-strung that she has difficulty calming herself even in the peace and quiet of her own bedroom. You must learn and then accept your baby's particular tension level. Just because your sister's baby is so laid-back that she slept through your baby shower doesn't mean that your child will be as mellow. Always err on the side of avoiding chaotic environments. If you continue to place your child in situations that overstimulate her you are looking for trouble.

Overstimulation can be overt (such as family gatherings where the unfortunate baby is passed around the room like a plate of hors d'oeuvres) or subtle (when well-meaning parents keep their child up too long after a feeding just to "play"). It may be difficult for you to refuse the request of a relative or friend to hold your new baby, but if your baby is high-strung you may have to do it anyway. Don't be afraid to make me the bad guy. Mention my name, refer them to this book, and tell Aunt Louise and Uncle Tom that you would love to let them hold the baby, but you have read that some babies become fretful and sleep poorly if they are handled by strangers. Tell them you are pretty sure their niece is one of those high-strung babies. Of course, you could always skirt the issue completely by telling them you are concerned about all the germs in the community.

You can always fall back on Wilkoff's Grandparent Rule, which states, "In the first two months of life only parents and grandparents should hold the baby." Of course, if you have a mellow baby who is resistant to overstimulation you can broaden the rule to include aunts and uncles, but be careful. Thoughtful and sensitive people who remember what new babies are about won't even hint at wanting to hold your baby, but there are still enough overenthusiastic relatives and friends around that you must be prepared to protect your baby's space to keep her well rested. Make your job easier by not inviting many (or *any*) guests to your house, and do your darnedest to avoid taking your baby to gatherings of any kind. Remember, in those first few months she should be sleeping most of the time, and when she is not sleeping she will be eating. This doesn't leave any time for entertaining guests.

Stay Close to Home

Unless you are blessed with one of those rare children who can and will sleep anywhere, you should plan on sticking close to home for the first three months at least. We want your baby to become comfortable with and attached to her home, her room, her crib, and her schedule. If you continue to disrupt her routine and ask her to sleep in strange places she may rebel by showing you her cranky side.

Trips out in public mean more opportunities to have your baby subjected to the overstimulating in-your-face behavior of rude strangers. Crowds often contain snotty-nosed toddlers who can spew millions of germs with one uncovered sneeze. Even breastfed babies are vulnerable to infections of all kinds, including colds.

While staying close to home for the first three months may sound very conservative, it is very helpful in keeping young infants well rested. It doesn't mean that little walks around the yard or the neighborhood must be delayed. If the temperature is safe, a little fresh air each day is good for everyone. But make sure that these little safaris don't interfere with the natural sleep patterns that you have been trying to encourage. A stroller or a baby-jogger is another way for your child to fall asleep. Make sure that your baby has chosen her crib or bassinet as her primary sleeping place before you begin taking her out for extended jaunts.

As often as possible, take turns babysitting at home so that your parenting partner can have some free time out of the house. Although it is hard to leave your baby with a sitter the first time or two, learn to make use of in-your-home child care to allow your child to enjoy the consistency of being able to sleep in her own bed. If your schedules and your pocketbook don't make these alternatives possible, make your trips out of the house with your new baby short and to the point. Try to schedule appointments around your baby's sleep schedule whenever possible. This is just one of the first examples of how moving your child's sleep needs up the priority list will make your lives and hers much more pleasant.

What About a Pacifier?

Once your baby has demonstrated that she knows how to gain weight consistently and will keep a pacifier in her mouth, you can consider including a pacifier in your sleep-management plan. By creating a few simple rules now when she is just a few weeks old, you and your child can enjoy some of the benefits of a pacifier while avoiding most of the negatives.

First, do not even consider the use of a pacifier until your baby is gaining weight consistently. This warning is particularly important if you are breastfeeding. In the first few days of life, a newborn is still trying to decide what and how to suck. If you offer your baby alternatives such as bottles and pacifiers when she is in this ambivalent stage, she may decide that she prefers them to her mother's nipple. This phenomenon is often called nipple confusion, and it happens so frequently that most breastfeeding advocates urge you to avoid a pacifier until you are confident that you and your baby are accomplished nursers. Once you are sure that your infant is gaining weight consistently (ask your pediatrician) and you can clearly identify her "I'm hungry cry" from her "I'm tired" or "I just want to suck" cry, then you can give the pacifier a try. Until that time, assume that when your baby is crying and wants to suck that she is hungry.

Second, let's agree that a pacifier is to be used only as a sleep aid. It is not a plug to stick in your baby's mouth to keep her quiet. If your baby is hungry, feed her. If she is uncomfortable, then soothe her. If she is tired, put her to bed. Don't just try to muffle her cry with a pacifier. Next, remember that we have already agreed that to keep things simple your baby should be sleeping only in her crib. Therefore, your child should only be given a pacifier when she is in her crib. Don't forget that raising a well-rested child is based on forming associations—good and logical associations. If your baby is going to use a pacifier, she must learn from the beginning that when she feels the need for her pacifier, that feeling is one of being tired, and that the place to be when she is tired is her crib or bed.

It is a very simple concept, but one that will guarantee that you won't have a toddler who wanders around all day long with "binky" stuck in her mouth. As your child gets old enough to ask for her pacifier, restate to her the rule that you have been following since before she was a few weeks old: "You can have your pacifier anytime you want, but you must be in your crib or on your bed."

When you can consistently identify your baby's fatigue cry, and decide to introduce a pacifier as a sleep aid, you may find that she is one of those newborns who can't create enough consistent suction to keep it in her mouth. It could take several weeks or even months. You may decide after a few days of getting up every few minutes to replace "the plug" that it isn't worth the effort.

Make Her Thumb Available

Thumb sucking is a more natural way for your child to pacify herself and put herself to sleep. We have all seen those pictures of a fetus sucking its thumb, but unfortunately it usually takes most babies at least three months or more to learn how to find and suck their thumbs. Parents often tell me that their children became better sleepers when they finally learned to suck their thumbs. If you want your child to at least have the option of using her thumb as a built-in pacifier, you must first create a situation in which your child has easy access to her thumb, and this means uncovering her hands. Many newborn nurseries and new parents (advised by well-meaning relatives) put little mitts on babies' hands so they won't scratch their faces. Obviously, this makes thumb sucking impossible. I suggest that you abandon the mitts and accept a few scratches on your baby's face.

> *It is difficult to clip a newborn's fingernails, and many parents, including myself, have accidentally clipped a bit of finger in the process. A safer and equally effective way of trimming nails is to use an emery board and selectively file only those nails that feel sharp. Don't try to nibble them down as some old wives and friends might suggest. It is no safer and may result in an infection.*

It still may take your baby four or five months to learn to suck her thumb, and some infants never learn how to do it. Don't worry that she may end up with braces on her teeth because she is still sucking her thumb when she is seven years old. This rarely occurs, and you will learn in Chapter 5 why a well-rested child is very unlikely to be sucking her thumb long enough to cause an orthodontic problem. For the moment all you can do is make sure your baby has free access to her thumb. Once she learns how to suck on it, think about creating a good association. In other words, if she isn't hungry, assume your baby's sucking means that she is tired and it is time to put her in her crib.

• • •

The steps are straightforward. First, make sure that your child is healthy and gaining weight consistently. Don't allow your baby to become overtired or overstimulated. Create a dark and quiet place for her to sleep, and then put her in her crib while she is still awake. It is her job to put herself to sleep. Your responsibility stops with making sure she is well nourished and has a safe and comfortable place to sleep.

To help you remember the basic philosophy behind this process, imprint this sentence in your brain:

Your baby should wake in the same place that she fell asleep.

Think for a moment what this means. If you allow your child to drift off in your arms as you pace the floor and then place her in her crib, when she wakes she will *not* be in the same place in which she fell asleep. If she hasn't slept an adequate amount of time, this will create a problem. If she awakens prematurely and is still tired, she is going to protest until she is returned to the environment in which she initially fell asleep. This means that you are going to have to crawl out of your bed, go to her room, pick her up, and pace the floor with her until she falls asleep. In other words, your sleep will continue to be interrupted as long as your child associates the process of falling asleep with the rocking motion of your body as you walk the floor.

From time to time all children will wake before they are fully rested. The more tired your child is the more often these premature arousals may occur. Unfortunately, this is just another case of the poor getting poorer. If you want to break this cycle, remember that sentence: *Your child should wake in the same place that she fell asleep.* That means not in your arms, at your breast, in your bed, on the couch, or in a swing. When it is time for your baby to fall asleep, place her in her crib, in her own room, while she is still awake. In the next chapter I will tell you what to do when she complains.

Summary of Strategies

- Make as many trips to the pediatrician as it takes to reassure yourself that your baby is healthy and gaining weight.

- Remember, it is *not* your job to get your baby to sleep. You need only provide the proper conditions.

- Whenever possible, put your baby to bed awake.

- Set a clear day-night pattern with lights-out at around 7 P.M. and on again at 7 A.M.

- Remember that your child should be sleeping most of the time.

- Avoid overstimulation. Playtimes should last ten to fifteen minutes at most.

- Continue to keep your life simple with a minimum of extracurricular and extramural activities.

- Don't use a swing to put your baby to sleep.

- Allow your child to sleep only in her bed.

- Keep feedings to less than twenty or thirty minutes (including burping).

- If your baby seems to need a pacifier, give it to her only when she is in her bed. Better yet, allow her access to her thumb.

- Your child should awake in the same place in which she fell asleep.

4

Making It Work

The first few weeks with your new baby have been chaotic. Labor and delivery were more exhausting than you expected. In spite of your careful planning to keep life simple for your family of three, even when you aren't exhausted you can't even think about getting anything done because your baby is so unpredictable. In this chapter you will learn how to establish healthy, long-lasting routines that are the basis of the solution presented in this book.

The Hard Part

In the last chapter I told you that if you wanted your child to be well rested he must learn to put himself to sleep in his own bed, preferably in his own room. Of course, this requires that you place him in his crib while he is still awake. It would be awfully nice if after you put him down he would look into your eyes, smile a little smile, close his eyes, and drift off to sleep. But life isn't always nice or easy.

Although some children will nod off quietly and sleep peacefully for a few hours, you must expect your baby to protest when you put him down. He may initially accept his crib without complaint, but after lying there for a few minutes he may have second thoughts and begin to cry. He may even sleep for half an hour, then wake prematurely and begin to fuss. What should you do when your baby objects to falling asleep in his crib?

First, you must be sure that your child is healthy and well-fed. If he is crying because he is sick or hungry, you must respond to those needs. Second, you must be absolutely committed to the idea that it is important—in fact, *very* important—for your baby to learn sleep independence. The next part of raising a well-rested child is one of the hardest, and to succeed you must be convinced that you are doing the correct thing. If you are a little wishy-washy about the concept, reread the last few chapters for strength, because the next thing I am going to tell you is to *let your baby cry himself to sleep.*

There, I've said it. You probably knew the bad news was coming but were hoping that I had some other secret up my sleeve, but unfortunately I don't. However, if you have followed the suggestions in the last chapter it won't be as difficult as you feared. If you have been careful to protect your baby from overstimulation and fatigue by staying close to home and keeping his life simple, he may not put up much of a fuss when you put him in his crib to sleep. By not allowing him to fall asleep in your arms or in a swing you have avoided some bad associations. Now it is time to help him form some good associations.

You may feel it is cruel to let your three- or four-week-old baby cry at all, let alone for the ten or twenty minutes it might take for him to fall asleep. You may have read that if you don't respond to his needs your baby will feel insecure. Someone may have even told you that by ignoring your baby's cries you are sending him a message that he isn't loved or wanted. The advocates of that philosophy often claim, "You can't spoil a baby." In principle I agree with their admonition that you must meet your baby's needs, but I don't think that helping your child to learn sleep independence has anything to do with spoiling.

It is your job to protect your child from anyone or anything that might harm him. You are responsible for seeing that he is properly nourished and taken to the doctor when he is ill. And if your baby is tired you must help him meet his need for sleep. This means providing him with a dark, quiet place that is protected from the weather, but it does not mean putting him to sleep. That is a process that he can and must learn to do for himself. Your responsibility stops when you have established the appropriate conditions.

When your child cries something is bothering him, and you must figure out what that something is. Is he hungry? Is his diaper wet? Is he is sick or is he simply tired? It may be difficult for you to believe, but fatigue can make your baby feel so uncomfortable that he will not only cry, he will shriek so loudly that you are sure he must be in pain. In fact, he may be in pain. As you will read in Chapter 6, migraine headaches so severe that they make a child vomit can be a consequence of fatigue. Infants can't tell us what hurts, but I suspect that many babies who are overtired have headaches.

Because you are new to this parenting thing, it will take you a while to learn which of your child's cries mean that he is hungry or sick or tired. Even if I came over to your place, I wouldn't be much help in determining the message behind each cry. They would probably all sound about the same to me, but after a few weeks of trial and error *you* will become the experts in cry identification.

For example, if your child has just been fed and burped, and you know he is gaining weight well, you can rule out hunger if he begins to cry. By checking his diaper you will rule out another cause. It is more difficult to be sure if your new baby is sick, because he hasn't been around long enough for you to be confident about what constitutes normal behavior. However, trust in your own hunches when it comes to your child's health. Maternal intuition does exist, and during my twenty-five years of practicing pediatrics I have come to rely on it heavily. Paternal intuition is less reliable, but fathers can also learn to sense when their children are sick before there are obvious symptoms. When you are in doubt, always check with the doctor.

I hope you will quickly discover that once you have satisfied your baby's hunger the most likely explanation for his crying is fatigue. If you aren't sure from your own experiences, please trust in mine.

> *If there is no other obvious explanation, your baby is probably crying because he is tired.*

Because your child cries when he is tired, and we believe that it is important for him to learn how to put himself to sleep in his own crib, you aren't being cruel if you allow him to cry himself to sleep. In fact, by doing so you are following the most logical alternative. Of course, your baby would rather be rocked to sleep cuddled in the warmth of your arms. Who wouldn't? During the last nine months he became accustomed to floating around in the darkness of a uterus filled with warm amniotic fluid. Accepting the realities of the outside world will take some time, but it won't take long. Many babies learn to put themselves to sleep in their cribs with nary a whimper, but even if your child objects loudly to the concept of independent sleeping, he will learn in just a few days . . . if you are consistent and persistent. Between crying spells your baby will begin to experiment with different body positions; he may even find his thumb. By putting him in his crib while he is still awake you are giving him the opportunity to discover some things he can do by himself that will make it easier for him to fall asleep. In other words, he will be creating associations that he will be able to use day after day, night after night, to put himself back to sleep when he is tired.

However, if you interrupt this learning process by picking him up as soon as he begins to cry it will take just that much longer. Think of it this way: When you place your baby in his crib you are saying to him, "You are tired and this is where we think you should sleep." He may lie there for a few minutes and decide that he would rather be sucking on a nipple when he is tired, and so he begins to cry. If you pick him up as soon as he cries you are in effect saying, "We're sorry. We didn't really mean what we said before. We'll rock you or walk with you and let you suck on our finger until you fall asleep. You can learn to put yourself to sleep some other time." But that other time may never come, or at least by the time it does come many months later you have become a sleep-deprived zombie. Remember, we want your child *and* you to be well rested. Allowing your child to cry while he is learning to put himself to sleep isn't cruel, but it can be difficult to do. Here are some suggestions on how to do it humanely and efficiently.

Cold Turkey and Ferber

Although you may still feel a little uncomfortable about letting your baby cry himself to sleep, I hope you are willing to give it a try. How long should you let him cry? Until about ten years ago many pediatricians would have answered, "As long as it takes, but at least twenty minutes." As you might expect, many parents found it very difficult to allow their children to cry this long, and so some never even tried. However, in 1984 Dr. Richard Ferber's best-selling book, *Solve Your Child's Sleep Problems,* was published. In it he criticized those of us who were suggesting to parents what might be called the "cold-turkey" approach. Instead, he recommended a more gradual approach that has since become known as "Ferberization." Although thousands of parents have found that Dr. Ferber's suggestions have been very helpful, I have found that some families may need to fall back on a modified cold-turkey approach to help their children achieve sleep independence. Let's start by seeing how you might apply the principles of Ferberization to your child's sleep patterns.

First, remember that you have done all those other things we talked about in the last chapter. Those preconditions are very important if you want to succeed quickly. But now your sleepy baby has begun to cry. Wait as long as you can before you return to his bedroom. If you are like most first-time parents this may be only two or three minutes. It is very hard to listen to children cry, but listening to your own child cry is one of the hardest things you will ever do.

When you go into the baby's bedroom, don't turn the light on. Your goal is to do as little as necessary to interrupt his crying. Begin by rubbing his chest to quiet him. If this isn't successful pick him up and pat his back gently. Say a few soothing words if you must, but don't initiate a "conversation." Remember, less is better. Next try some walking and rocking, but don't turn the light on and don't leave his bedroom. If you begin to wander around the house your baby may become overstimulated, and new and unwanted associations can develop. Resist the temptation to feed your baby to stop him from crying. Remember, we have already decided that he isn't hungry. He's just tired, and he is learning how to put himself to sleep.

Once the crying has stopped, it is time to put him back in his crib. *Do not wait until he falls asleep before you put him down!* If you allow your baby to drift off while you are rocking him in a rocking chair, you are creating another bad association. Remember, we want him to learn to put himself to sleep in his own crib, not in your lap. If he happens to fall asleep in his crib while you are rubbing his belly, that isn't great, but it isn't that bad either. At least you have created one very good association: sleep = crib. The rubbing will become unnecessary in just a few episodes.

When he has stopped crying and is back in his crib, leave the room. If he starts to cry again, even if it is before you have left the room, allow him to cry for five minutes longer than you did initially. When you return to his room follow the same procedure you did the first time. If he begins to cry after this second trip add another five minutes to your waiting time and continue this gradual increase until your baby remains asleep. If you get to the point at which it has been two hours since the last feeding, you can offer to feed him and then start the process all over again. However, if your baby falls asleep after two or three minutes of sucking it was a mistake to offer the feeding, because you have just enabled a bad association. Chalk that up as a learning experience and try to hold out a bit longer the next time.

If each time you go in to settle your baby down he seems to cry more vigorously, you may want to consider trying to let him go cold turkey. Sometimes if Ferberization doesn't work it might be because your intervention confuses or overstimulates the baby. Often this can be avoided by sending Dad in for the calming session. Particularly if your baby is breastfed, he is less likely to expect his father to feed him until he falls asleep. However, if this doesn't work you may want to try letting your baby cry for at least twenty minutes, or up to an hour, before you go in the first time. Most new parents can't hang on long enough to make this cold-turkey approach work, but if you can do it, go for it. Some older children who are having trouble getting to sleep may require many hours and many nights until a new habit is established. However, if your baby is less than three or four months old I don't recommend going much longer than an hour. It will usually take just three or four nights for your baby to learn how to put himself to sleep in his own crib. If at first you don't succeed, take a few days of rest, reread the last few chapters, and try again. Some experts don't recommend trying this kind of sleep management for a child under four months of age, I guess because they feel it doesn't work. However, I have found that it can be done very successfully when parents understand the process and can create an environment that encourages good sleep habits.

How to Survive the Wait

None of us enjoys listening to a child cry, but there are a few parents who feel that they absolutely can't tolerate the crying. Some parents have told me that it even made them feel sick. If you are one of these unfortunate people, it may help to get involved in some chore or activity that can create a noise buffer, such as vacuuming or running the hair dryer. Don't make the sound so loud that you can't hear any sound your child may make. Just create a minor noise distraction to make waiting a little easier. Now you can understand why it is helpful to have your baby sleeping in a separate room with a door.

If your spouse obviously just can't listen to your baby cry, offer to assume the role of bad guy for the few hours or days that it may take for your baby to learn to put himself to sleep. Suggest that your partner leave the house if that makes it easier. It is nothing to be embarrassed about. We each have our own strengths, and some people just can't tolerate their child's cry long enough to effectively mold sleep behavior. Talk about the problem between yourselves and figure out how the more cry-tolerant parent can be available during the critical learning period.

You both must agree that it is the correct thing to do. You can make the process a little easier by writing a little contract of exactly how long you are going to wait with each episode before you go in to settle your baby (see sample contract on page 63). Although I have suggested five-minute intervals, you may find that this is too long for you. That is fine. It is much more important that you agree and are consistent and persistent. Helping your baby develop sleep independence is important, but it is much more important that your family remain intact. While the behavior of a sleep-deprived baby can cause friction between parents, we don't want the cure to be worse than the problem. Don't allow your attempts at Ferberization to cause so much squabbling that your marriage suffers. If you can't agree on how to manage your child's sleep, begin by speaking to your pediatrician. Don't be afraid to talk to a marriage counselor if you feel that your relationship is in jeopardy.

Colic, a Case of Being Tired and Gassy

The problem starts with defining the term "colic." Since it does not exist as a specific medical diagnosis, everyone seems to have his or her own definition. Most pediatricians agree that there are some babies who have frequent episodes of intense crying or crankiness that are not easily explained or remedied. Fortunately, the behavior is usually outgrown at about three months of age. To minimize confusion let us call that vaguely defined condition Colic with a capital C. Although there is agreement on the issue of whether there are children who exhibit this collection of symptoms, there is really no consensus as to its cause or management.

On the other hand, physicians can agree on a definition of the adjective *colicky*, with a small *c*. The term is used to describe pain that is very intense but short in duration. For example, the pain associated with passing a kidney stone or gallstone is colicky. The gas cramps and discomfort you may experience while you are having a bout of diarrhea are colicky. The pain that a woman feels during labor can be described as similar to colicky pain in that they are both brief and intense, although labor pain can be much more severe.

<u>Sample Contract</u>

We agree:

- That it is important for our daughter, Rachel, to get an adequate amount of sleep.
- That it is important for her to learn to put herself to sleep in her own bed in her own room.
- That to learn sleep independence she may at times need to cry herself to sleep.
- That if she is healthy and well nourished it is humane to allow her to cry.

Furthermore we agree:

- To put her in her crib awake whenever possible.
- If she begins to cry we will wait _____ (five is suggested) minutes before we return to her room.
- We will do the minimum necessary to settle her crying and then return her to her crib awake.
- If she begins to cry again we will wait an additional _____ (two is suggested) minutes before we return to repeat the process.
- We will continue to repeat the process, adding _____ minutes, until she falls asleep on her own.
- If the process has not been successful after ninety minutes, we will feed her again and start over.

Signed:_____(her mother)

_____(her father)

_____(date)

There are numerous causes of colicky behavior in infants. Intestinal upset due to cow's milk or lactose intolerance is one. Gastroenteritis (commonly known as stomach flu) is another common cause of colicky abdominal pain. The pain associated with an ear infection could have a colicky quality. There are a myriad of other less common conditions such as glaucoma or angina that, believe it or not, can occur in infants and cause colicky pain.

With all of these potential causes for colicky pain in infants you can see why it might be a serious mistake to label a fussy baby as having Colic with a capital C without first considering one of these specific, and possibly treatable, medical conditions. Therefore, before you or anyone else labels your baby as having Colic, the baby should be taken to the pediatrician for a physical examination and a careful consideration of the medical conditions that could be giving him episodes of colicky pain (notice the small c). Before you submit your child to any home remedy or old wives' concoction, give the pediatrician a chance to look for some specific medical condition that might be causing the problem. The pediatrician may not be able to find a diagnosis to explain your baby's colicky behavior because most colicky babies defy our attempts at explanation if we confine ourselves to the usual medical diagnoses.

Then why are there so many colicky babies? The vast majority of children who have colicky symptoms and in whom medical causes have been ruled out are sleep deprived. An exhausted infant is usually a cranky infant and may have episodes of crying so intense that you are sure there must be some physical cause for the pain.

This concept is difficult for many parents to accept, but twenty-five years of observing infants and children have convinced me that fatigue can create behavior indistinguishable from the pain we associate with more obvious causes such as ear infections or being stuck by a needle. As you will read later in this book, sleep deprivation in older children can cause specific pain syndromes such as headache and leg cramps. An infant, who obviously can't speak, may also have some specific pain such as headache or abdominal cramps associated with his fatigue.

If you have ruled out a medical problem and are convinced that your child is getting the proper amount of sleep and rest, you may be dealing with what I might diagnose as Colic (note the capital C). These unfortunate infants swallow more air than they can burp out and then must suffer the consequences as that gas works its way through the intestinal tract. Most of the gas that troubles babies is swallowed air and not somehow manufactured by the complex chemical processes in their intestines. There are certain circumstances in which gas is formed by difficult-to-digest substances that a baby has ingested such as lactose. However, these occurrences are infrequent and most of the gas is just plain air that went in the top end of the digestive system during feeding, crying, or nonnutritive sucking (pacifiers and thumbs).

Gas Management

Your infant will burp more easily if he is awake. If he is too tired he won't burp adequately and will suffer later for that air he has swallowed. When your baby is sleep-deprived he may cry more and swallow more air, creating more pain. Those gas pains may interfere with his sleep, and the cycle of fatigue, air swallowing, pain, fatigue, air swallowing, etc. etc. goes around and around. Burping early and often in the feeding may help. Changing the position and technique of burping may help. Experimenting with different kinds of bottles, nipples, and nipple holes may help. Simethicone drops given by mouth to reduce bubble size in the stomach and intestines may help. Colic won't subside until your child learns to swallow less air and burp on his own. These skills usually don't develop until an infant is about three months of age, but it does occur—if you can hold on that long.

Unfortunately, your child could have both Colic and fatigue. These two problems are often intertwined and can feed off each other. Again, just as the rich get richer and the poor get poorer, if your baby is overtired he will be less tolerant of pain in general and the gas pain of Colic in particular. Just think of your own experiences. If you are well rested and stub your toe you may utter a few expletives, but if the injury comes at the end of a long day it will probably bring you to tears.

When I have been able to help families manage a child with Colic, the solution almost always involves a combination of gas management and fatigue prevention. Colic can be a frustrating problem. It will get better on its own, but you may be able to speed the improvement by close attention to the fatigue-prevention skills you have read about in Chapters 2 and 3.

What About a Crib Vibrator?

A few years ago a couple of pediatricians developed a mechanical system to manage colic. It was based on the observation that many infants will sleep best in a moving car. Their machine consists of a vibrator that attaches to the springs of the crib and a noise generator that creates a soft hum. The combination is tuned to make the baby think his crib is a car in motion.

The concept makes sense as a sleep aid if we are willing to accept the fact that it encourages an association between sleep and a mechanical contraption that might stop working without warning. The equipment seems safe, and the manufacturers claim good results. I have recommended it to some families who were finding it difficult to follow Dr. Ferber's or my usual recommendations. However, too few of my patients have used them for me to comment on their effectiveness.

Crafting a Good Bedtime Ritual

The foundation of a good bedtime ritual begins before birth with the steps I have outlined in Chapter 2. It continues with helping your child to reach the second milestone, learning to put himself to sleep in his own bed in his own room, but it is during the second year of life that the ritual should be developed to its fullest form. Of course, the characteristics of the ritual will probably change as your child gets older. It is likely that one of you will still be involved in putting him to bed until he is at least ten or eleven years old, when your child will develop his own rituals that no longer require the participation of a parent. However, I know many teenagers who still have trouble settling down to sleep without help from their parents. The basic issues of when, who, what, and how long it is going to take to get your child to sleep need to be addressed as infancy is ending. The answers to those questions should help you build and reinforce a good bedtime ritual before you face the challenge of the twos. If you succeed they won't be as terrible as you have feared.

We adults have our own bedtime rituals to help us make that transition from being awake into that refreshing, but sometimes scary, state of sleep. We brush our teeth either before or after we get undressed. We may get out our clothes for the next day. We go to the bathroom. We may take a shower or bath. We may or may not say a prayer or meditate. We may read a book or watch TV or listen to the radio. We arrange our pillow just so and open or close the window. For some of us these rituals are so important that if anything is the least bit out of order we will have great difficulty falling asleep.

Sleep rituals allow us to gradually wind down from full activity to sleep. There is security in routine, and for many of us going to bed is the first time in the day when we have felt alone, physically alone, alone with our thoughts, our fears . . . and the dark. It can be scary, even for grown-ups. The routine, the repetition, and the familiarity of a ritual can help us relax and allow sleep to take us. We are confident that we will wake again the next day, because we did everything just the way we did it the night before. Some of us, on the other hand, are so exhausted at the end of the day that the only ritual we need is assuming a horizontal posture, and we are off to dreamland.

For children, the comfort given by a good sleep ritual is extremely important to make that sometimes frightening transition to being alone at night. Your child is still dependent on you for all sorts of things. The reassurance offered by a ritual can help him accept the inherent insecurities of being alone in a bed in a darkened room.

Children thrive on routine and consistency. If you are successful in creating a good bedtime ritual during your child's first year or two, it can be modified as the child gets older, but it will retain its therapeutic value for many years. A comforting and consistent bedtime ritual is one of the cornerstones on which a family is built.

When?

The timing of your child's bedtime is one of the most important health issues you will face each day. Unfortunately, many children go to bed too late. How should you select a healthy bedtime for your child? A place to start is with the table from Richard Ferber's book that appears on page 18. Figure out what time your child needs to get up in the morning for your house to function successfully, then subtract that amount of time from the table and you will arrive at the approximate time at which your child should be asleep. Of course, you should also subtract the amount of time the ritual takes. If it takes you 45 minutes to complete your child's bedtime ritual and he should be asleep by 7:30, then you must start the process at 6:45.

Here in Maine we tend to be early risers. The major employer in our area of the coast starts at 7 A.M., and of course the lobstermen are out on the water long before that. High school is already under way by 7:30. Therefore I recommend to parents that they have their preschoolers in bed by 6:30 or 7, and school-age children by 8 P.M. Junior high and high school age children may be able to last until 9 P.M., but for a child who is active in sports (or other extracurriculars) this may be too late. These may seem like early times to you, but twenty-five years of experience have shown me that the families who ignore these guidelines are the ones who are more likely to experience a variety of fatigue-related problems.

If your community tends to get going later than we do here in Maine, you could push these suggested bedtimes a bit later. If you have to wake your child in the morning, then his bedtime is too late. If your child is cranky most of the time, he probably needs to go to bed earlier.

Parents often complain that my suggested bedtimes are too early for their child because he doesn't seem to need as much sleep as other children. Although there is wide variation in the stamina of children, most parents underestimate how much sleep their children need. Before you consider a later bedtime you must be able to honestly say that your child is happy, successful, and healthy—and that you are rested and have enough time for yourself.

Who?

Who should be the adult involved in the bedtime ritual? There would seem to be an obvious answer to this question: his parents. Not so simple. It is an important role for parents, a very important role, but sometimes parents' work schedules conflict with their child's bedtimes. While I think it is extremely important for at least one parent to be part of the bedtime ritual, *it is not necessary that both parents be involved every night.* It is more important that your child have a healthy bedtime than it is for him to see both of his parents at bedtime. This is a principle that lies at the heart of raising a well-rested child. It is up to you as a parent to reprioritize your schedule if you want to be part of the bedtime ritual. As a team you need to organize your lives so that at least one of you can be there for an appropriate bedtime, but it does not have to include both of you.

By taking turns at the bedtime ritual, you will build some flexibility into the system so that either one of you can be effective in getting the child to bed. This will allow each of you to do evening activities out of the house without ruining the bedtime routine. In addition, sharing bedtime duties begins to build into the ritual the notion that some other adult can become the surrogate parent. This may it easier when you are ready to have a babysitter take over your role in the ritual. Making yourselves interchangeable parents for the bedtime ritual can be difficult, particularly if work schedules dictate that one of you must become the primary put-to-bedder, but a little ingenuity and persistence can help. Sometimes it may require that the primary tucker-inner actually leaves the house (a sham) so that there will appear to the child that he has no alternative. Each parent can have his or her own particular variation of the bedtime ritual. This kind of variety is only natural. However, be careful to emphasize the similarities in your different routines so that the transitions can go more smoothly.

If one of you can't be home until after your child's bedtime, resist the temptation to wake him when you return. I know that may seem like an obvious warning to many of you, who, as I do, believe in the old adage about letting sleeping dogs (and children) lie. However, there are many parents who sort-of-accidentally-on-purpose wake their child with a kiss on the forehead when they finally get home at night. Certainly, I don't want to be accused of telling parents not to kiss their sleeping children, but if it interrupts your children's sleep, don't do it. Kiss them twice in the morning.

What?

What should a good bedtime ritual include? It should not include elements that might be stimulating. Fathers, in particular, often promote physical activities such as wrestling, hide-and-seek, and tickling. A bath is often included in the extended bedtime ritual. However, for some children a bath can become too stimulating and interfere with the wind down to a restful sleep. If your child is having trouble getting to sleep, these kinds of activities should be eliminated not only from the bedtime ritual itself but also from the pre-bedtime period.

Food and drink should not be part of a bedtime ritual for various reasons. Although there is some evidence that milk may contain an ingredient that encourages sleep, drinking too much of anything can interfere with sleep. This is particularly true if your child drinks a large amount of fluid and then is wakened by a wet diaper or the urge to urinate. Second, good oral hygiene dictates that your child's teeth should be brushed after eating and before going to bed. Finally, some scientists suspect that calories consumed late in the day are more likely to accumulate in our bodies as fat. Therefore, a bedtime snack might be a contributor to obesity and is to be discouraged. Even if your child is on the thin side now it is still a good idea to discourage evening snacking.

The traditional elements of a bedtime ritual are songs and stories, and many families include a prayer. These oral traditions should begin long before your child can understand the meaning of the words. As he gets older bedtime can be a time of sharing, with the child and parent relating some of the special parts of the day. However, it is obviously not a time to deal with touchy issues that are not going to be resolved on the spot and may only serve to agitate your child so he can't fall asleep. For example, it would be unwise to wait until bedtime to bring up a discipline problem that had occurred earlier in the day.

It is very important to have a consistent pattern to the bedtime ritual. Children feel more secure when they can count on having the same elements in their ritual night after night. Once your child is a bit older it is important to include the child in the process of deciding what elements to include and in what order. Your child might try to drag the ritual out, either because he enjoys it or because he merely hopes to delay what for him is an unpleasant transition. It may be necessary to write down a list of the acceptable elements and their order. For the preverbal child this may be done using pictograms. Here is an example:

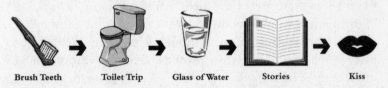

| Brush Teeth | Toilet Trip | Glass of Water | Stories | Kiss |

This will give you a sort of contract, something in black and white, that you can point to if your child tries to stall at bedtime. If your child requests a night-light, keep it small and dim. Sometimes the shadows a night-light creates can cause more problems than the light solves. If music has become part of the ritual, make sure that it is soothing and limited. It is very likely that your child will try to add as many elements as he can come up with to his bedtime ritual because he doesn't want to be left alone. Sleep specialists often call this problem "sleep refusal." Chapter 8 will give you many more suggestions of how to keep the ritual short and to the point and how to manage sleep refusal.

Finally, although I have emphasized the importance of consistency when it comes to developing a bedtime ritual, you must be prepared to be flexible as your child's interests change with age. Usually you will get tired of reading the same story every night long before the child wants to change the routine. Hang on, your efforts at creating and maintaining a good bedtime ritual will help your child make that important transition into what can be that frightening realm of night. With an effective bedtime routine in place your child will be able to get to sleep at a healthy time, which will allow him to start the next day well rested.

Security Objects

Does a well-rested child need a security object? The answer is an emphatic "Yes!" However, to maximize its benefit you must institute and then enforce some simple and sensible rules. The late Charles Schulz gave us "Peanuts," a neighborhood of cartoon children and pets who fortunately never seem to grow up. We can laugh at their innocent observations and sympathize with them when their peers treat them shabbily. Charlie Brown, Lucy, Pigpen, Snoopy, and Woodstock speak for all of us. However, Linus, his blanket slung over his shoulder, has always held a special place in my heart. More than anyone else in the Peanuts gang, Linus is a tragic figure, and he provides us with a lesson on how not to use a security object.

Why does he carry that ratty old blanket everywhere he goes? Is he insecure? Are his parents terrible losers? What is missing in his life? I know the answer, and the tragedy lies in the fact that Linus's problem could be solved so easily. Like hundreds of thousands of other children in this country, what Linus is missing is . . . you guessed it . . . sleep.

For decades, blankets, teddy bears, dolls, and scraps of cloth have been labeled security objects. More recently, the term "transition object" has become popular among psychologists and specialists in child development. However, neither of these terms adequately describes the primary function of such objects. Linus's blanket is first and foremost a sleep aid. When he was three or four months old he began to associate it with the pleasant sensation of drifting off to sleep. Along with his thumb, it became an integral part of the support system that he clung to as he mastered sleep independence.

After he learned to walk, he began to nap less consistently. When he felt tired the blanket that had helped him fall asleep was a comfort. His parents allowed him to carry it around because if they didn't he was cranky and irritable. Because he could have his sleep aid with him whenever he wished, he didn't need his bed for his naps. He could curl up on the floor for a five-minute catnap or wander around like a half-asleep zombie. Instead of being fully awake or completely asleep, Linus found that he could wobble around with the older kids in the Peanuts gang in a sleep-deprived stupor.

Of course, his blanket could also provide him comfort when bad and scary things happened. It had been there for him when he was learning to put himself to sleep, and it did make him feel more secure when he fell and bumped his nose. And these little accidents happened quite frequently because he was always tripping on the frayed satin binding that always trailed at his feet. However, Linus found that his blanket was still most helpful as he fell asleep at night and during the day when he was tired.

Unfortunately, although a cartoon character can function well on little sleep, your child cannot. In many ways a sleep aid is similar to a pacifier, and many of the same rules apply.

- Encourage the development of a sleep aid by moving your child's blanket with him whenever he is going to sleep in a different location (at day care, at Grandma's house, or in his car seat on a long trip).

- Don't allow the sleep aid to be used in any other setting (in a swing, on the couch, or on short car trips).

- As your child begins to walk make it clear that his sleep aid must remain in his crib.

- Allow your child to have his sleep aid *anytime* that he wishes, *but* he must be in his usual sleeping place (crib, bed, or sleeping mat at day care).

- An exception to the rule is a long (over an hour) car trip when you would expect him to sleep.

- When a traumatic event such as a trip to the doctor's office is anticipated, bring the sleep aid along. Keep it out of sight in a diaper bag until it is needed.

The philosophy behind these guidelines is one that I introduced way back in Chapter 2 when I suggested that you keep your newborn's life simple by making logical associations that linked eating, sleeping, and playing with specific locations. Remember that during those first weeks we wanted him to sleep in only one place to avoid confusion as he was learning sleep independence. We want your child to retain that association because it will encourage him to keep good sleep and nap habits. You can't make him sleep in his crib or bed, but you can discourage him from sleeping in other places by restricting his sleep aid to his bedroom.

By allowing him to have his sleep aid anytime he wishes you are offering him the chance to rest whenever his body feels tired. Sometimes you may miss the subtle signs of his fatigue, but when he asks for his blanket you will know that he is getting tired. By limiting where he can have his sleep aid you will encourage him to keep that positive association with his bed. If you permit him to wander around with his sleep aid like Linus, your child is more likely to give up his naps prematurely and stay up past his healthy bedtime because he has catnapped all day. By making it very clear that whenever he feels tired he has a place to go where he can use his sleep aid, you will discourage him from wandering around in a fog of fatigue.

On long car rides you expect your child to sleep, and so a sleep aid is permitted. For rides of less than an hour your child should be able to stay awake easily. If he repeatedly falls asleep or begs for his sleep aid on these shorter rides, he is probably already sleep-deprived, and you should be looking into doing some rescheduling.

At day care the same rules should apply. Make sure the provider understands that your child is allowed to have his sleep aid whenever he wishes, but that he must be in his sleep area. If he is asking for his sleep aid all of the time, it probably means that he needs more sleep, but it also may indicate that there is something about the day care environment that is troubling him and making him feel insecure. It may be time to ask questions about peer interactions, staffing changes, or other variables that may be upsetting your child.

Although your child's blanket or teddy bear is primarily a sleep aid, it can also provide him some extra comfort when things are going badly. When your child falls and bumps his mouth, you can expect him to request his sleep aid even though he isn't tired, because it also is a security object. It would be inhumane to forbid him this comfort. This is one of the reasons that you should allow your child to have his sleep aid whenever he wishes. It is the nice thing to do. However, to avoid confusion you should still require that the sleep aid be kept on his bed. You can offer to accompany him to his room and sit on his bed with him while he holds his special object. When he has recovered his composure and is ready to venture out in search of excitement once more, the blanket remains behind, waiting for the next collision to occur.

These guidelines may sound rather arbitrary at first, but remember that you are providing your child with free access to his sleep aid/security object. The only restriction you are placing on its use has to do with location. If you are consistent in applying these simple rules, you will find that your child will be not only well adjusted but well rested as well.

Daytime Napping

From Chaos to Predictability

Once your baby has learned to put himself to sleep in his crib, both you and he should be getting some much-needed rest. However, his feedings, and therefore your opportunities to sleep, probably won't be coming at predictable times. Although some babies feed every four hours like clockwork, most newborns, particularly if they are breastfed, are erratic. They may sleep for two hours between some feedings and four or five hours between others, often without any obvious pattern.

First, you must accept this unpredictability as one of the rules of the parenting game, just as you must realize that during the first month or so your baby may at times need to feed as often as every hour and a half. However, there are some strategies you can employ to convert this chaos into a routine that will allow you to once again have a life. With a predictable pattern in place you can begin to think beyond survival and even get some real sleep.

For the first two or three months your child's day will consist of between six and ten sleep-feed-awake cycles. The sleep periods may be as short as an hour and a half or as long as six or seven hours. The feedings should last no longer than half an hour. The awake periods should be no longer than twenty minutes during the first month, but may creep up to forty or forty-five minutes in length by the time he is four months old. On the opposite page are graphs of what three typical days might look like.

Notice that each day is different, except that from 7 at night until 7 in the morning the awake time has been reduced to zero. This will occur if you have been careful to feed your child in his bedroom with the lights out and have resisted the temptation to play with him during this period. By establishing a distinct day/night pattern and an early bedtime you have begun to create order out of chaos.

Unfortunately, you can't control the length of his sleep periods because you can't make your baby sleep any longer than his body intends to sleep. However, if he has a premature waking that is less than an hour from his previous feeding, you should allow him to put himself back to sleep even if it means letting him cry. Don't accept these mini-naps without a struggle. In the long run, short little catnaps won't allow either of you to be truly well rested.

These repetitive sleep-feed-awake, sleep-feed-awake cycles should eventually evolve into a routine that has distinct and predictable naps. This process will usually occur naturally as your baby begins to sleep longer between feedings. This may first occur at night. He will also develop more stamina and curiosity about his environment and be able to remain alert and cheerful for more than fifteen or twenty minutes after a feeding.

You can build more predictability into your baby's life by initiating specific activities at the same time each day. A bath, a short walk outside, and a few baby gymnastics are just some of the fun things your baby can anticipate will happen on a schedule. Time these activities to occur at periods in the day when experience has told you he is likely to be awake, but be careful to avoid overstimulation just before you expect him to be winding down for sleep. With these fixed guideposts in his day, your baby's sleep-

Six-Week-Old's Chaos

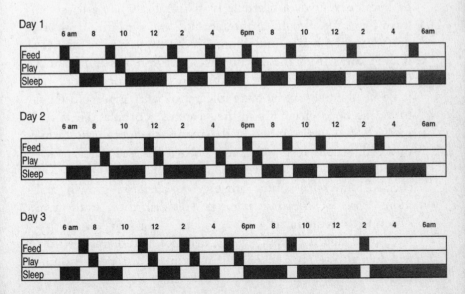

Four-Month-Old's Routine

awake pattern will become more predictable. As he goes from a bath at 9 A.M., a walk at 2 P.M., and lights-out at 7 P.M., he will begin to develop his own schedule, and distinct naps will begin to appear.

If you will be returning to a job outside the home, your baby will have to follow your work schedule, and initially you may need to wake him in the morning. While it is usually not a good idea to wake your child, sometimes it just has to happen. He will adjust rapidly as long as he is given adequate opportunity to sleep during the rest of the day.

By the time your baby is three or four months old he should have settled into a daily routine that includes three or four distinct and relatively predictable naps. If this hasn't happened it may be because your own schedule is still erratic. If some days you leave for work at eight in the morning and on other days you don't leave the house until noon, this can confuse your baby. He doesn't know if it's Tuesday or Thursday. He hopes and assumes that each day is going to be a carbon copy of the one before.

Some children can be quite tolerant of what appears to them to be the unpredictability in their parents' schedules. However, most children will respond to day-to-day changes in their routine with erratic sleep and cranky behavior. Researchers at Purdue University have observed that children raised in noisy or chaotic homes have more anxiety, less cognitive growth, and more delays in acquiring language skills than those from more structured environments.

Certain aspects of your life just may not lend themselves to a schedule, at least not a schedule that an infant or toddler can understand. Tuesdays and Thursdays may have been long days in your office well before you were hired. Your aerobics class may meet only three days per week. However, strive to make each day appear to be a clone of the one before to your baby. For example, if you are offered the choice of working five five-hour days or three eight-hour days each week, the five-day workweek will be less disruptive to your child's sleep routine.

Even though you can't make your days exact copies of one another, keep your child's napping schedule high on your family's priority list. This will become easier as he falls into a pattern of three, and then two, distinct naps. As he gets older, work hard to make appointments and plan activities that will fall during the longer awake intervals. Strive to give his naps the highest priority as you plan your schedule.

From Three Naps to Two

By the time your child has reached his first birthday he will be taking only two naps each day. He may have achieved this feat as early as his fourth month, or he may be seven or eight months old before it happens. Each child's sleep maturation progresses at its own pace, and there is a wide variation of normal. However, the two-nap milestone comes at about the time children are taking three solid meals per day. This usually will occur at around five and a half or six months of age. By that time most babies have enough stamina to stay up for more than an hour and a half after their breakfast feeding. After a one-and-a-half-hour or two-hour morning nap they are ready for some play time and then lunch, after which they go down promptly for another two-hour nap.

There are no hard-and-fast rules to guide you through the transition from three to two naps because there are just too many variables. Don't rush the process. If your six-month-old gets cranky after he has been up for only forty-five minutes in the morning, then you just have to put him down to sleep even if it means he will still be having three naps a day. On the other hand, if he is only catnapping for half an hour at a time, you should use Ferberization or the cold turkey approach to help him back to sleep. Although the evolution from the relative chaos of your six-week-old's sleep-feed-awake, sleep-feed-awake cycle to a predictable two-nap schedule will occur primarily as the result of natural forces, you may need to tinker a little with the process to help it along.

Selecting Sleep-Friendly Day Care

If both you and your spouse have jobs outside the home, you can't ignore the role that day care will play in your child's sleep patterns. For example, the day care you select must be able to provide an environment in which your child can get some sleep or rest when he needs it. Here are some suggestions to help you evaluate your day care options from the perspective of fatigue prevention.

Ideally, you will have several day cares to choose among. A site visit is a must, and you should visit each place several times, with at least one visit scheduled during nap time. Here are some things that are important to consider as you visit day cares and interview providers. Obviously, they all have to do with sleep. You will also be looking at many other issues, including cleanliness, safety, and cost.

Where Will Your Child Sleep?

Your infant should have crib. Does it meet current safety standards? Your toddler doesn't need a bed, but he should have a mat to soften the hard floor. Can the sleeping area be made dark and quiet? If there is a broad range of ages, some of the children may no longer nap; will they be disrupting your child's sleep? Is the sleep area cool enough? Or too cold?

What Is the Sleep/Nap Schedule?

Children under the age of one should be offered at least two nap periods. If there isn't any routine that includes time for naps, you should look at other day cares. Does the afternoon nap begin so late that your child will still be sleeping when you arrive to pick him up? This, of course, will make it hard for you to put him down at a healthy hour at night.

Can the Schedule Be Flexible Enough to Meet a Variety of Sleep Requirements?

Some children need more sleep than others. Will your child be able to sleep longer if he needs the rest? For example, if he is a little bit under the weather but not too sick to go to day care, will your child have the option of taking an extra rest on his mat? Some day cares may not have the space or staff to allow for this degree of flexibility. If there are older children who don't need naps, will their activity disrupt your child's sleep?

Is the Atmosphere Hectic or Relaxed?

When children congregate noise happens. Each child's supply of playful energy can feed off his playmates' and multiply to the point of exhaustion. However, architecture of the day care and the management style of the provider can influence the degree to which youthful enthusiasm can progress to chaos.

Will your child be able to escape to an oasis of quiet when the play has become too frenetic? If not, you may find he is exhausted and complaining of headaches when you pick him up at the end of the day. Does the day care provider attempt to create a balance between healthy physical activity and quiet times in which the children can recharge their batteries, or does the place always seem to be spinning out of control? Avoid the latter.

Does Size Matter?

In general, one might think that a larger day care would be more hectic and less flexible, but this may not always be true. The philosophy of the day care provider, the room layout, and the staffing arrangement may be much more important in creating a sleep-friendly atmosphere. A small home day care with only three children that is run by someone who doesn't understand the importance of naps and healthy bedtimes may be more exhausting for your child than a large day care with fifty children that gives sleep and fatigue prevention a high priority.

Does the Day Care Provider Put Sleep and Rest High on Her Priority List?

Ask! Enter into a dialogue about sleep. Has she read this book? Did she agree with its basic premise? Did the day care provider have trouble with sleep problems in her own children? Ask her what they were and how she solved them. Does it sound as though she will be able to get your child down for naps easily? If it sounds as though she won't give your child's rest and sleep their proper emphasis, look elsewhere.

How Does the Location Fit into Your Commuting Schedule and Your Child's Sleep Routine?

Will the travel significantly disrupt your child's sleep schedule? For example, will you be forced to wake your child so that you can travel an extra forty-five minutes to get to his day care? Remember, if you must wake your child he isn't getting enough sleep. Is the day care so out of your way that by the time you have picked up your child and driven home you have only an hour to feed him dinner and get him to bed? Commuting time with your child can't really count as quality time. An hour saved on your travel time is an hour that you can spend together or that he can use for some much-needed sleep.

Maybe You Can Afford Day Care in Your Own Home

After you have visited all of the day cares you are considering, and before you choose one, you may want to think about one last option: day care in your own home. If you are unsure whether any of the day cares you have seen will be able to keep your child well rested, you may want to investigate the possibility of hiring someone to come into your home. This arrangement can give you more control over your child's sleep schedule, diet and activities. By providing the day care in your own home you can be sure that your child will be sleeping in his own bed. You can give specific instructions about schedules and your philosophy about sleep and rest. Sometimes this can be an expensive option, and you may not think of yourselves as a family who can afford a nanny. However, by offering another family or other families the chance to bring their children into your home to share the sitter you have hired, you can cut the costs. Of course, as you bring in more children you may acquire some of the disadvantages of a larger group setting.

I realize that in many if not most parts of this country good, reliable day care can be extremely difficult to find and expensive when you do find it. With a limited number of affordable options to choose from you may have to make some compromises I have not anticipated. However, I urge you to keep your child's sleep needs high on your list of priorities as you consider the various options you have identified.

If you don't consider your child's sleep needs when you select a day care, you leave yourself in the position of picking up a very cranky child at the end of your workday. Group activity for a child can be a lot of fun, but it can also be fatiguing. We are all bound to be a little off our best at the end of the day, but remember that your time with your child may be limited to those waning hours of his day. It seems to me that you would like your child to be reasonably rested when the two of you get together. A day care arrangement that hands you an exhausted and underslept child at the end of the day isn't doing either your child or you a favor.

On the other hand, I know of many families who have found that their children actually sleep better in the more structured atmosphere of a well-run day care. On the weekends, the novelty of having both Mom and Dad around to play with may be so stimulating that you will have difficulty getting your child to nap. Day care can be a very positive influence in helping you raise a well-rested child. However, you may have to hunt around for a while to find a sleep-friendly facility.

Taking the Show on the Road

I have already cautioned you that if you want to keep your new baby well rested you should keep him pretty close to home for the first three or four months. It may take at least that long for him to reach that second milestone of learning to put himself to sleep in his own crib and then to develop a predictable napping pattern. Remember, children thrive on routine, and leaving home—even for just a few hours—can be upsetting for a child who is still learning sleep independence and trying to form a strong attachment to his crib.

However, we live in a mobile society and have become dependent on the automobile and the airplane to maintain our friendships and family connections. Eventually, the pressure to visit grandparents or the desire to get out of the house to socialize with old college roommates will force you to take this well-rested baby of yours on the road. Although a few infants seem able to sleep at any time, in any place, you must expect your baby's sleep patterns and his behavior to deteriorate when you shake up the status quo by taking him on a trip. His crib and his daily routine are things he has come to rely on for comfort and security.

Can you still keep your child well rested when you are traveling? Yes, you can, but it isn't easy. I don't care who you are, traveling is exhausting. One of the perks of being an author is that occasionally a publisher will send me on tour to promote my books. Media escorts meet me at the airports and take care of all the arrangements. They put me up in nice hotels, and I eat at good restaurants. I need only remember to put one foot in front of the other. It couldn't be easier, but it is still tiring, and I always need a day or two after I get home to catch up on my sleep. You must keep in mind that when you travel you and your baby are going to become fatigued. You can and you should plan to prevent it, but despite your best efforts both of you will become overtired and cranky from time to time. However, here are some suggestions that can help you all stay as well rested as possible.

Make a Sensible Itinerary

Your child still needs naps and a healthy bedtime to stay rested and pleasant. You must keep this in mind as you plan flights, rest stops, visits, and social engagements. If you fail to leave sufficient time for rest and sleep, I can guarantee that you will have a cranky child and a miserable trip. I realize that the airline carriers did not consult you before they scheduled their flights from Philadelphia to Denver, but whenever possible you should choose an itinerary that is the least disruptive to your child's sleep and nap routine.

Break the trip up into segments that will allow you and your child to get some rest. Keep the schedule of appearances and social obligations light on the first day and night after you arrive. Grandparents are not only eager to see their new grandchild, they want to show him off to friends and relatives. Warn them ahead of time to keep the schedule reasonable, particularly the first day after you arrive. Give them an idea of when the baby will be napping, and remind them that he is just a little child and so has a bedtime that is around 7 or 7:30. For example, make it clear that taking your four-month-old out to a restaurant for dinner at 8 or planning to visit with Aunt Louise until 9 in the evening is asking for trouble.

Although it may make you appear rather compulsive, you might ask your hosts to describe what they have planned for your stay. Don't be afraid to speak up if the schedule of events sounds too hectic or conflicts with your baby's sleep schedule. If you begin this dialogue long before you leave on your trip, there is much less risk of feelings' being hurt and/or your child's becoming so fatigued that every day is an ordeal. Warn your hosts that you are raising a well-rested child and this means that you consider his sleep a high priority. Hearing this should help them adopt realistic expectations of what your visit will be like.

Grandparents want to see and show off a cute and happy grandchild. It's too late to do much about the cute part, but at least make it clear that a reasonable and age-appropriate schedule of events is mandatory if they want their friends to see their grandchild on his best behavior.

Don't Leave Home Without Them

If your child has adopted a pacifier or a blanket to help him fall asleep, bring it along. Long trips are a time to bend your rules about sleep aids. Plane rides, car trips of more than hour, and long days away from home in strange places are occasions for unlimited use of blankets and pacifiers. If your child is tired, and despite your best planning you find yourself without a place for him to sleep, at least he may be able to doze in your lap with the help of his blanket or pacifier. Sleep aids can sometimes save the day when it has just gotten too long for your sleep-deprived child. The trick is to make sure that it is back to business as usual when you have returned home or there is a bed available. If you don't reestablish the only-in-your-crib rule for sleep aids promptly, you can lose one of your best allies in the battle to keep your child well rested.

Start the Trip Well Rested

You know that traveling is going to be tiring, so start out when you both are well rested. You wouldn't think of leaving for a long car trip with only half a tank of gas, and you shouldn't consider taking your child to his grandparents' house when he has missed a two-hour nap and gone to bed an hour late the day before. I know this can be difficult because there is always some last-minute running around that must be done before you leave on a trip. However, if you leave on a trip with an already sleep-deprived child you are looking for trouble. You are guaranteed to have a cranky traveling companion. It is equally as important that *you* depart in a well-rested state. Your patience and emotional stamina are going to be tested at every turn in the journey. If you want to be an effective and cheerful parent, you must not be burdened by a sleep debt that you incurred before the trip even began.

Look at your family's schedule. Make sure there aren't any late nights planned for either you or your child for the three or four days before the trip. Cancel meetings or ask to be excused. Eliminate any obvious wrinkles in your child's schedule that might interfere with his naps or bedtime. Think of yourself as an athlete preparing for the big game. Plan ahead; be prepared so that you and your child can go to bed early the night before you leave.

Will There Be Room at the Inn?

Getting there is only half the fun. Make sure the sleeping arrangements at your destination will be adequate for you and your child. If you are going to be in a motel or hotel, you may not be able to afford a suite that will allow you and your child to sleep in separate rooms. Of course, this may be a problem. Your presence will probably disturb his sleep, and his wakings will interrupt yours. Just do the best you can do. Try some creative redecorating using bedspreads and furniture to at least provide a visual barrier between you and your child.

If you are staying with friends or relatives, tactfully but forcefully explore all the sleeping options in search of one that will allow your baby to have a space of his own. This will be important for naps as well as night sleeping. If you broach the subject when the visit is still in the planning stages, your hosts will have more time to come up with a solution. While your sleep is important, it is more important that your child be well rested, and you might suggest some arrangements that aren't quite optimal for you but allow your child a better chance of getting a good night's sleep. In other words, when sleep is concerned, if compromises are to be made, I suggest that you make them rather than your child.

Ideally, your hosts realize that babies cry and that tired babies are more likely to cry. Beg their indulgence and tell them that sometimes you may have to allow your child to cry himself to sleep. On the other hand, you are a guest and there are limits beyond which your child's screaming will wear out your welcome. It is probably unreasonable to expect your hosts to tolerate the thirty- or forty-five-minute-long crying spells that may be required to remind your exhausted child that it is his job to put himself to sleep. However, some grandparents remember what it was like and may be willing to trade some crying the first night or two for a happy and well-rested grandchild for the remainder of the stay. But first you need to ask them if it is okay.

You may have to bend some of the rules that were so helpful in getting your newborn to learn sleep independence. Remember, you will only be away for a week or so, and you can all climb back on the sleep wagon once you get back home. If your hosts or the people in the adjoining motel room can't tolerate the crying, you can try rocking your baby to sleep. As a very last resort you can take your child into bed with you. I have told you that these are bad habits to get into, but sometimes you just gotta do what you gotta do. We can hope that all the work you have done in the first few months has created such a well-rested child who has become so skillful at putting himself to sleep that these extraordinary measures won't be necessary.

Jet Lag

If your trip involves crossing more than one time zone, you and your child will encounter the effects of jet lag as your internal time clocks struggle to reset themselves. All of the strategies I have just outlined can help minimize the ill effects of jet lag.

Starting off well rested, planning a reasonable itinerary, and finding a sleep-friendly environment once you have arrived are extremely important. Following Ben Franklin's advice about early to bed and early to rise will help the adjustment come more quickly. In other words, resist the temptation to sleep late the morning after you arrive. Force yourselves to get up, but don't plan a strenuous day. Deal with the inevitable fatigue by going to bed early, and the next day will go better for you and your child as your biorhythms adjust to the new time zone.

It's Not Over When It's Over

Unfortunately, your child may not reestablish his good sleep habits as soon as he finds himself back home in familiar surroundings. In fact, I often receive calls from parents whose children seemed to sleep well while they were traveling and then begin to have trouble settling back into their usual routines. Of course, if your baby has become accustomed to sleeping in the same room or even the same bed with you when you were in strange places, these bad habits must be discouraged promptly on your return.

The first step is to accept that sleep disruptions after a trip are normal and to be expected. In addition to his fondness for communal sleeping, your child is probably tired from the traveling and so may have more arousals and awakenings. The second step is to immediately reinstitute the basic sleep rules. No more co-sleeping. Everyone back in their own rooms and in their own beds. If your child is old enough to articulate a complaint, you merely need to explain (once) that when you were traveling the rules had to change, but now that you are home it is back to business as usual.

You may have planned for some quiet recovery days at home after the trip, but regardless, begin immediately to reinforce the good bedtime rituals you had instituted before. You may need to use the gradual techniques of Ferberization or even resort to the more difficult cold turkey approach. Whichever method you employ, start it as soon as you get back home. Don't delay the inevitable.

• • •

Traveling can provide wonderful learning experiences for your child, and it can offer him opportunities to establish bonds with his extended family. However, traveling can be exhausting, and unfortunately, many family trips don't live up to expectations because some parents fail to plan adequately for their children's sleep needs. Disappointed grandparents who were eagerly anticipating a visit from their grandchildren are happy to see the cranky and exhausted little demons leave. Regardless of whether you are taking your new infant to visit his great-grandmother for the first time or taking your four-year-old to see Disney World, plan ahead and arrange a reasonable itinerary that will allow everyone to get plenty of sleep. Your well-rested child can be a pleasant traveler as long as you don't allow him to become too sleep deprived.

Summary of Strategies

- If your baby is well fed, appears healthy, and is crying, he is probably tired and needs to be put to bed.

- It may be necessary to allow your child to cry until he falls asleep.

- Draft a written contract if you and your spouse differ on how long to let your baby cry.

- Don't label your child as having Colic until he has been evaluated by a pediatrician and you are confident he is getting enough sleep.

- Craft a bedtime routine that is efficient and consistent, and start early enough to assure that your child will fall asleep at a healthy hour.

- Select a sleep-friendly day care that will work with you to foster good sleep habits.

- When planning a trip, make sure that you and your child will be well rested when you leave, that you both will have adequate sleeping arrangements when you arrive, and that your itinerary is realistic and takes into account your child's sleep requirements.

5

YOUR WELL-RESTED BABY IS GROWING UP

The challenge of establishing an efficient and effective bedtime ritual that allows your child to fall asleep at an appropriately early hour is behind you. Naps are now predictable and long enough to assure that your child's total dose of sleep is adequate to keep her healthy and happy. Your child has mastered putting herself to sleep in her own bed, although this is a skill that may have to be relearned many times over the next few years.

On the other hand, your child may already have celebrated her first birthday before you started reading this book. Although I suggest that you eventually read all the chapters, this is a particularly good place to jump in. You have not burned any bridges behind you, and there are plenty of opportunities to apply the sleep solution to your particular situation.

This chapter will help you keep your child well rested as she makes the transitions from crib to bed, from two naps to none, and from home to school.

From Crib to Bed

Keeping your toddler well rested will require you to respond appropriately to the many transitions that accompany her growth and development. For example, she is getting bigger and more agile; when should you move her out of her crib and into a bed?

The answer is simple: When she starts risking injury by climbing out. There is no other reason I can think of to upset the status quo by initiating the transition yourself. In fact, if your child is so well coordinated that she can safely climb in and out of her crib, let her sleep there as long as she prefers it.

Don't worry that she will develop curvature of the spine because she has outgrown the space. It won't happen. Peer pressure and her natural desire for independence will force her into a bed long before her posture is in jeopardy.

There are several reasons to delay the move from crib to bed for as long as you can. The first is that if you have been successful in helping your child to develop healthy sleep habits, she probably has formed a rather close emotional attachment to her crib. Along with a blanket or stuffed toy, it has become one of her sleep aids/security objects.

My wife and I discovered this fact when Emily, our second child, was born. We thought it would make perfect sense to move her two-year-old sister, Jennifer, into a bed. What a mistake! Jennifer, who had always been a good sleeper, began to wake frequently and, of course, in her sleep-deprived state became uncharacteristically cranky. Welcome to the real world, Young Dr. Wilkoff!

The trauma of suddenly having to share her parents with a new sibling was hard enough, but having to face it without the comfort of her favorite sleeping place was just too much to ask of poor little Jennifer. We borrowed another crib for Emily for the six months it took her sister to decide that she was ready for a big girl's bed. Don't underestimate the emotional investment your toddler has in her crib the way my wife and I did.

Another reason to delay the transition to a bed is that the crib provides you with some degree of control over where your child is during naps and bedtimes. Until she learns to climb over them, the four barred walls of her crib prevent your toddler from wandering around the house when she has awakened prematurely. Don't give up this control until concerns about your child's safety force you to move her to a bed.

How to Make the Shift

Your child has learned to get her leg over the crib side, but she isn't agile enough to safely make it to the floor. She begins to climb/fall out. To keep her from conking her head or breaking her collarbone, you will need to move her into her bed.

A mattress on the floor may be all that you can afford, and it is all that your child really needs. However, if you want to buy a bed, make sure it isn't too high off the floor or install a side rail to prevent her from rolling out of bed in her sleep.

Next you need to create some form of security system to prevent your toddler from taking advantage of her newfound freedom and roaming around the house in the middle of the night. Usually she will come to visit you in your bedroom. She may want to climb into your bed, or she may just ask you to tuck her back into her bed again . . . and again . . . and again.

To manage these nocturnal wanderings, you will need to provide some sort of deterrent. If your toddler is not much of a climber, you may find that a gate across her doorway will serve the purpose. However, if your child has already demonstrated her gymnastic abilities by climbing out of her bed, you may need to latch her door. Many parents worry about the safety of this approach. It doesn't really bother me, but if you are concerned you may want to attach a bell to your child's door so that when she opens it in the middle of the night you will be awakened. This could be a traditional mechanical bell or a high-tech ringer patched together from parts you can buy at the local do-it-yourself electronics store. Whichever technique you choose, make sure that you do something. Although your child's repeated trips into your bedroom may be a nuisance, her explorations into more dangerous parts of the house such as the kitchen or bathroom must be prevented.

If the transition out of the crib is followed by night awakenings and calls for comfort or assistance, there are two approaches. The first is to ignore her requests; eventually (after three to seven nights) they will subside. Although this may be a strategy you are eventually forced to employ, it is probably more humane to go into your child's room to provide a little reassurance until she becomes comfortable with her new bed. Using the techniques discussed in Chapters 3 and 8, you should remain in her bedroom only long enough to be sure that she has stopped crying. If the protest resumes, wait two or three minutes longer before you return to quiet her. Continue to gradually increase the waiting time. Your child should respond to this Ferberization technique after three or four days, but it may take a week. If you discover that your child becomes more upset each time you return, you may need to resort to going the cold-turkey route and just allowing her to cry herself out. This is not fun, but sometimes Ferberization doesn't work as efficiently as we would like, and staying out of the room is the better answer.

If your child refuses to remain in her room, you may be forced to latch the door. The first time you do this return after thirty seconds or a minute, because she may be frightened and surprised that you would actually take this drastic step. However, once she knows you mean business she will probably agree to stay in her room if you promise not to latch the door. This technique is neither cruel nor damaging to your child's psyche. It is effective if done properly and emphasizes that you are a confident parent whose words can be believed and whose threats are followed by consequences.

Don't worry if you find your child asleep on the floor. If you have provided her with warm pajamas and enough blankets, she will be able to keep herself warm. She is perfectly capable of building herself a nest on the floor. When she discovers that she prefers the feeling of sleeping in her own bed, she will probably stay in bed after you have tucked her in.

It is important to make this transition from crib to bed as swiftly and smoothly as possible. Don't force it before your child is ready, but when the time is right don't waffle. Stick to your guns. Make extra sure that you keep your child's schedule mellow during this transition because both you and she need to be rested. Remember, the more tired she becomes the more likely she is to waken and then wander around looking for you—or trouble.

The Not-So-Terrible Twos

What an unfortunate stereotype—a three-foot-high demonic monster who must somehow be tolerated until she magically reaches the age of three. The "terrible twos" is a horribly unfair term. Of course, two-year-olds are adventuresome and curious. Of course, they are going to explore the borders of their environment and test the limits of their parents' authority, but they are my favorite age group. They are developing physical and verbal skills at warp speed, and they are fleshing out the skeleton of their personality. They are fun! It is sad that so many parents find the challenges of their two-year-olds overwhelming and give up any attempt at management, hoping to just ride things out until the "stage" is over.

If you want to enjoy your child's journey from one to three you must continue to place her sleep needs at the top of your priority list. Your well-rested two-year-old may be a handful, but she won't be terrible. Over my last twenty-five years in pediatric practice I have come to realize that terribleness in two-year-olds is the result of one or two simple problems. The first is the sleep deprivation created by the premature loss of one or both of the child's naps. The second is the failure by parents to meet the child's passion for exploration with a set of reasonable age-appropriate limits and an effective discipline program.

Paradoxical Hyperactivity

The challenges of nap preservation and limits setting can be made even more difficult by the confusing phenomenon I call "paradoxical hyperactivity." Common sense suggests that as a child gets more tired he or she will begin to slow down and become less physically active, until the child just curls up and goes to sleep. This may be true for some children, but many children become hyperactive as they become more fatigued. These unfortunate children will exhibit a shortened attention span, and they may become more aggressive and impulsive as they get more tired. The term "running out of steam" makes no sense when it comes to these children.

The key in managing this problem is to recognize that it is occurring. I often hear parents describe their children as not needing much sleep and, in fact, able to gain strength as the day goes on. Very often these parents are describing a case of paradoxical hyperactivity. Once the problem is understood, the solution is to intervene early and get the child down for a nap or bedtime before she gets wound up. If you have waited too long your child will be so overstimulated that it will be very difficult for her to fall asleep.

Although paradoxical hyperactivity usually first appears in the second year of life, it can persist all the way through childhood. Some children become so active and impulsive when they are tired they may be mislabeled as having ADD or ADHD (Attention Deficit Disorder or Attention Deficit and Hyperactivity Disorder). Chapter 6 explores the association between fatigue and Attention Deficit Disorders in more detail.

Healthy Napping

Even children whose parents have set good limits and used a simple discipline system to enforce them may become terrible two-year-olds. The reason is that many two-year-olds are allowed to give up one or both of their naps prematurely. The resulting sleep deprivation takes its toll. A tired child is a cranky child, a whining child, a child who throws tantrums—and may be an angry child. It goes on and on. In summary, a tired child is terrible.

It is natural for your child to give up her naps as she gets older. Many one-year-olds are still taking a morning and afternoon nap, but by age two most children are down to one nap in the afternoon. Some unfortunate children are already down to one nap a day by age one and may try to trick their parents into letting them get away without a nap at all. However, if you want your child to continue to be well rested the answer is simple: *Don't let her give up her naps.*

> *If you want your child to continue to be well rested, don't let her give up her naps.*

This may be easier said than done. Here are some suggestions that can help you keep your child from dropping her naps prematurely.

Weld Lunch to the Afternoon Nap

If you form a tight linkage between lunch and her afternoon nap, you make it more difficult for your child to give up that nap prematurely. Just think about it for a moment. Your child is never going to give up her lunch. In fact, for most children it is the favorite meal of the day. If you have created a schedule and an atmosphere that fosters a close bond between your child's nap and that midday meal, you will be helping your child develop and keep a good sleeping habit. When your child has become accustomed to the lunch-nap, lunch-nap, lunch-nap routine month after month, it will be more difficult for her to imagine any less-healthy alternative.

As your child finishes the last bite of her peanut-butter-and-jelly-sandwich she should be immediately ushered off to her room for a rest/nap. You may want to read her a short and boring story, but don't allow other activities to creep in between the midday meal and the nap. You don't want to run the risk of your child's becoming overstimulated and therefore less likely to be able to settle down for a rest.

You may be tempted to take your child with you to the store to run "just a little errand" after lunch. Don't do it. One thing is bound to lead to another, and her nap will be forgotten—or even worse, your child will doze off in the car for what will be an incomplete and insufficient nap. Without an adequate nap she will become tired and cranky late in the afternoon or fall asleep shortly before dinner. This mistimed nap will throw her (and your) nighttime schedule completely out of whack. You will both pay a heavy price in fatigue and misbehavior.

We all have a natural tendency to become sleepy in the middle of the day, particularly after we have eaten a meal. Take advantage of this biologic fact of life and weld your child's nap to her lunch. If you wait until she begins to look or act tired it may be 3 or 4 in the afternoon. By that time, if she takes a one- or two-hour nap she will be waking just a couple of hours short of her healthy bedtime. This out-of-sync nap will make it very difficult for you to get your child to go to sleep at night because she will have re-paid enough of her sleep debt that she won't be tired enough to settle down at an appropriate bedtime. If you have to wake her the next morning, she will certainly start the day sleep-deprived, and you can look forward to a day full of misbehaviors.

> *Take advantage of your child's natural tendency to become sleepy after a midday meal and put her down for a nap immediately after lunch.*

The principle is very simple. Form an association between your child's afternoon nap and a permanent fixture in her life, her lunch. Her biologic clock will tell her that this is a natural time to sleep, and the bond with her favorite meal will discourage the unfortunate and premature disappearance of her naps.

Going from Two Naps to One

Maintaining a tight connection between lunch and the afternoon nap is also an important concept to remember when your child seems on the verge of downsizing from two naps to one. The situation is a classic "damned if you do, damned if you don't." If your child is allowed to drop one nap she is likely to be so fatigued that her behavior will be unmanageable. However, if you can get her down for her second nap she may not be tired enough at her usual bedtime and will be up charging around until all hours of the night. These are truly the horns of a dilemma, and failure to resolve the problem means that the horns will be worn by the little sleep-deprived devil who will be making life miserable for you and herself.

The first question you must ask yourself is "Is it really time to drop one of the naps?" If your child doesn't seem very tired in the morning or she seems very resistant to going down after lunch when she has had a morning nap, it is probably time to give up one of her naps.

Unless your child awakens or must be awakened very early in the morning, the afternoon (from here on let's use the more ac-curate term, *"after-lunch"*) nap is the one to retain. There are chil-dren who seem very fatigued by 8:30 or 9 in the morning, and these children should probably still be taking two naps per day. If your child fits into this category it might simply be because she came into the world with a natural sleep requirement that is above average. However, I often discover that this situation is best managed by instituting an earlier bedtime and/or creating more calm in the child's schedule by shortening her stay in day care or weeding out activities that may be overstimulating.

The Floating Lunch

When you have decided that the handwriting on the wall says "It is time to drop the morning nap," the next step is to make sure you still have that one remaining nap welded tightly to lunch. This close association will allow you to employ the "floating lunch" strategy. This simply means that you vary the timing of your child's remaining nap by giving her lunch earlier or later, depending on how tired she appears on that particular day. Re-member that because you have created an after-lunch nap you can dictate when her nap begins merely by choosing when to serve lunch. This concept gives you better control over your child's daytime sleeping schedule and provides you with the flex-ibility the unpredictability of toddlers demands.

> *If you have created an after-lunch nap, you can dictate when your child's nap begins merely by choosing when you serve lunch.*

Here's how it can work. Let's say that your two-year-old daughter, Karen, is having a good day. After a short trip to the grocery store you and she go to the playground. You bump into one of her buddies and they have a wonderful time making mud-pies in the dirt. You arrive back home at 11:45. Lunch is on the table by just before noon, and she is down for her nap by 12:30.

The next day, on the other hand, doesn't go quite as well. Karen wakes with a new runny nose. She may even have a little fever, but she eats her usual breakfast, and you decide that it is safe to take her to her usual Wednesday morning playgroup. Things go pretty well initially, but you can tell that your daughter doesn't have her usual patience with Margaret's characteristic aggressive-ness. Karen begins to whine, and by 10:15 she is asking to sit in your lap instead of playing with the other children.

Obviously, your child is getting tired. More specifically, sick and tired. It takes energy to fight off an illness, and Karen's new cold is beginning to sap her strength. Her usual stamina will allow her to remain happy and functional until nearly noon, but not today. She has lost her steam, and it isn't even 10:30 in the morning.

What should you do? Tell the other mothers that you hope they enjoy the muffins you baked. Scoop up Karen and head straight home. As soon as you get there, announce, "It is lunchtime," even though it's only 10:50. Slap together her favorite peanut-butter-and-jelly-sandwich and sit down with her while she eats. When she is finished she already knows it is nap time because that's the event that always follows lunch. By 11:20 Karen is drifting off to sleep, more than an hour earlier than her usual after-lunch nap. Although she went down early she actually sleeps fifteen minutes beyond her usual wake-up time. This is another clue that she is sick and needs more rest. She goes to bed at her usual time and wakes the next morning with a full-blown cold, but seems to have regained her usual stamina and cheerfulness.

This example of how to apply a "floating lunch" to the situation in which your child is sick is fairly obvious. In fact, you may have applied the principle yourself before you ever picked up this book.

Remember that stamina varies from child to child and from

day to day. Sometimes the cause is obvious: illness, staying up late to watch a television special, playing hard all day on the first warm day of spring. However, some days, even some weeks, we are just more tired than usual. Maybe we are fighting off some little virus that has produced no other obvious symptoms. Maybe it has to do with phases of the moon or the amount of sunlight falling on our faces or some as-yet-undiscovered biorhythm. The bottom line is that it happens, and you and I don't have the time or energy to figure out why. The important thing to recognize is the fact that your child is tired and needs more rest. If you have established an after-lunch nap you have the perfect tool to deal with your child's fatigue, even though you may not know why she needs more rest on any given day.

As soon as you see your toddler showing signs of tiredness, stop whatever you are doing and make lunch. Remember, she can't tell time. Lunch is when *you* say it is, and her nap will automatically follow. Don't worry that the nap (or the lunch) is too early. Usually, she will sleep longer than usual because she is over-tired. If she doesn't sleep very long, merely put her to bed earlier than usual in the evening.

Complications

Although these complimentary concepts of the floating lunch and the after-lunch nap sound very logical and simple, they may not always be easy to apply. What happens if your child is in day care? Is it too much to ask your day care provider to put your child down for her nap immediately after lunch and feed her lunch early if she is looking tired? I don't think so.

We have already explored the challenge of finding a day care that is sympathetic to the problem of fatigue and sleep deprivation. I hope you have been able to find a day care that is flexible enough to accommodate the fluctuations in your child's day-to-day sleep needs. Ideally, lunch for a toddler should come at around 11 in the morning so that she can be down for a nap by 11:30. This kind of schedule makes good sense for the children of working parents who have probably been up since 6 or 6:30.

If you find that your child is exhausted to the point of being unmanageable or dysfunctional when you pick her up, and the day care provider seems unable to manage her naps appropriately, you may have no choice but to change day cares. I know this is not a step you will take lightly. It may be very difficult to uproot the status quo, but remember how important it is to keep your child well rested. Don't forget how many other aspects of her life and yours depend on her ability to get a healthy amount of sleep.

Occasionally your schedule or a sibling's schedule will make it difficult to float lunch earlier for your toddler. Sometimes you just have to be creative. You can keep a "lunch" of nonperishable items in the car so you can allow your child to eat in the car as you are driving home from an unfortunately timed appointment. Although this can create a considerable mess in the backseat, it will allow you to put her down for her nap within minutes of driving into the garage. The half hour you have saved may not seem like much, but it may be enough to make the difference between having a child who is just a little tired and one who is seriously fatigued.

As your child is passing through the awkward stage when she is going from two naps to one, it can be tempting to try to take advantage of your morning freedom and plan too many errands or activities. Keep the late-morning schedule light and flexible so that when you see your child getting tired you can beat a hasty retreat for home and her after-lunch nap. Be patient. As she gets older and develops more stamina you will be able to float lunch later and later.

But Don't Let That Remaining Nap Slip Away!

One of the most important principles of raising a well-rested child is to resist with all of your might the forces that can erode that precious after-lunch nap. As your child grows older she will gradually need less sleep. However, most parents underestimate how slowly this transition occurs. Turn again to Dr. Ferber's chart on page 18 to refresh your memory about how many hours your child should be sleeping. Of course, there is a wide range of normal. Many children still take a two-hour nap when they are in kindergarten, and some two-year-olds can do very well with only a one-hour nap. However, when in doubt assume that your child needs more sleep than she is getting. I bet that you will be correct 90 percent of the time.

> *When in doubt, assume that your child needs more sleep than she is getting.*

Dropping a nap isn't something that should happen suddenly, because your child's sleep requirements don't change overnight. There will be a very long period of time during which your child may not seem to need her nap for two or three days in a row and then on the fourth day have an emotional meltdown from fatigue. For months or possibly years your child's stamina is going to fluctuate from day to day. Some days she will require a nap and other days she will be able to sneak by without one until the evening bedtime. What is the best way to manage this unpredictable fact of life?

The Siesta Concept

Remember, our bodies are programmed to become tired and sleepy around noon. In many other parts of the world societies have traditionally preserved an hour or two after the midday meal as an oasis not only from the heat of the day but also from the hubbub of life. In Latin cultures it is called a *siesta*, and businesses and shops close down for a few hours so that everyone can get some rest if they feel they need it.

Incorporating a siesta into your child's schedule can be a very effective strategy for dealing with the frustrating transition period during which your child is moving inconsistently from one nap to none. It is really just a variation of the after-lunch nap. If you have successfully forged a strong bond between lunch and a nap you can take advantage of this association by converting the nap to an after-lunch siesta.

For you the process consists primarily of a change in attitude. You continue to take your child to her room after lunch, but instead of expecting her to sleep your goal is merely to provide a quiet environment in which she can rest and recharge her batteries. On some days she may take full advantage of this opportunity and fall asleep for an hour or so. However, most of the time she may just play quietly in her room. After an hour you can allow her to resume her other activities. We can't really call this a nap because she doesn't always sleep, but you have set aside a period of time in the middle of the day for rest and recovery. The nap has become a siesta.

Creating a siesta may not always be as easy as taking your child to her room for some quiet play. If she isn't feeling particularly tired you may have to work at establishing a relaxing atmosphere, but it can be done, and it must be done if you want your child to remain well rested. Unplug the phone. Turn off the TV. Hang a Do Not Disturb sign on the front door. Resist the temptation to make appointments at the dentist's or the hairdresser's during the two hours after lunch. Pretend you are in Guadalajara. In fact, you might appreciate the opportunity to take a little siesta as well. If you feel that you "must be doing something," do something that is sedentary and relaxing. Put some soothing music on the CD player and sit down and write letters, or send E-mails, knit, read, or paste pictures in a photo album. Remember, you must set the tone. Your behavior is critical to the success of the siesta concept.

Even if you have tried your best to create a restful atmosphere after lunch, your child may be unwilling to stay in her room for her siesta. In that case you may need to be more actively involved in the process. For example, sit down with your child and read several stories, preferably ones devoid of action and excitement. Whenever I read to my children, I could never resist the urge to yawn. The reading seemed to naturally relax me, and that usually rubbed off on the kids.

Although I have cautioned you against sleeping with your child, the siesta is an exception to this rule. An after-lunch rest period is so valuable in the process of raising a well-rested child that I believe little harm will be done if you agree to lie down on your child's bed for a shared nap. Of course, it is not your first option, and you must make it very clear that your child will not be coming into your bed, nor will co-sleeping carry over to become part of her evening bedtime ritual.

Video Naps

Like many pediatricians, I feel that the television-viewing habits of our children are seriously interfering with their health. The physical inactivity associated with watching TV is already taking its toll on the fitness of both children and adults and is a major contributor to health problems such as obesity and diabetes. However, if your child is not buying the siesta concept despite your best efforts at creating a mellow and rest-inducing atmosphere, "the tube" may be the answer. As distasteful as it may be for me to suggest such a thing, you might try sitting your child down in front of a nonaction video for an hour or so. At least one study has demonstrated that television viewers burn only slightly more calories per hour than they do when they are sleeping. Although this may not be good news for those of you hoping to lose weight by watching television, it does demonstrate that "tubing out" is very similar to sleep and may provide your child with a chance to recharge her batteries.

This video nap could be done sitting next to you on the couch, as though you were reading your child a story. However, I understand how tedious this might become if you were forced to watch the same *Mr. Rogers' Neighborhood* rerun several hundred times. Please don't extend this technique to the point where you are using television as a baby-sitter. Your involvement in your child's television viewing is very important. However, if your child is one of those who won't sit still while you are reading her a story, then try a video nap to help you preserve her siesta. As you will learn in Chapter 10, television is often one of the causes of sleep deprivation for the school-age child. The video nap may be the only situation in which TV can prevent fatigue.

When It Is Lost for Good

Eventually your child's after-lunch nap and then her siesta will disappear. This tragedy probably won't occur before her third birthday, and it may not happen until she is six. Despite your best efforts at welding your child's afternoon nap to her lunch and creating a siesta atmosphere, the time will come when you can no longer count on her to take the time for a little quiet R&R. On most days she will have the stamina to make it past dinner before she begins to show symptoms of fatigue, but there will be many days when she runs out of steam at 4:30 or 5.

If you put her down for a nap at that point you will mess up her nighttime sleep schedule. If you wake her for dinner she probably won't eat it, and then you will have a difficult time getting her back to bed at her usual bedtime. The better solution is to quickly fix her dinner and put her down for the night, even if it is only 5 or 6 o'clock. Don't worry about the quality of the meal. Try to include all four food groups, but ease and speed in preparation are more important than nutritional value. Most children this age have already done most of their serious eating early in the day, and they usually just spend dinnertime rearranging the food on their plates. Although I am a strong advocate of family meals, it is more important to get your exhausted preschooler to bed than to have her sit down at the table with her parents and siblings.

You may be afraid that by putting your napless child down early she will wake too early. Although this may happen, it is much more likely that she will get up at her usual time. Even if she does wake a little earlier, this early-to-bed solution is still the best answer for the child who has given up her naps and siestas but still occasionally becomes overtired. If you attempt to keep her up until her usual bedtime, you are robbing her of the opportunity to repay her sleep debt.

If your napless child refuses to eat her early dinner or falls asleep while you are preparing it, don't sweat it. She isn't going to starve overnight. Carefully move her to her bedroom and allow her to sleep through until morning. If she wakes before you go to bed, you could offer her a glass of milk or juice, but do not fix her a meal. Tomorrow is another day, and she will eat enough to make up for what she missed by going to bed earlier.

Tantrums and Misbehavior

Even a well-rested two-year-old wants to explore the borders of her environment. She will find trouble if it is around . . . and it always is. A thorough discussion of discipline is beyond the scope of this book, but I will say that I am a strong proponent of the "time-out" method. Reasonable limits that emphasize the child's safety and the integrity of objects that can't be moved should be put in place. When the child has transgressed, she is placed in her room with the door closed (latched, if need be) until she has been quiet for two minutes (or one minute per year of age). Some of you will cringe at the thought of latching the door, but failure to have control of the situation means that there is no effective discipline. You might worry that by putting the child in her room you will make the bedroom into a prison. Children aren't stupid. They understand that it is their removal from the family area that is important, not that they are in their bedrooms. Children are perfectly capable of enjoying their bedrooms as places to play even though the bedroom is also the place where they are sent when they have misbehaved.

An important added benefit of using your child's bedroom for time-outs is that most of the time when she is misbehaving, your child is overtired and often will fall asleep while she is serving her sentence. This additional nap may have a therapeutic value in that your child will finish the time-out more rested and therefore less likely to resume her dangerous or antisocial behavior.

Children as young as nine or ten months of age can throw tantrums, but the behavior really begins to flourish in the one-to-three-year-old age group. It is very clear to me that many children who have tantrums are doing so because they are overtired; when they become well rested the frequency of the tantrums will decrease dramatically.

The traditional recommendation given by several generations of pediatricians has been to simply "ignore the behavior." Although this is still good advice, it is incomplete and difficult to follow. Few parents have the courage and confidence to leave a two-year-old thrashing on the floor for the several minutes it will take for the tantrum to pass. However, if you are one of the lucky few who can turn a deaf ear to a child's screams of anger and frustration and walk away from the situation, do it! It will work.

On the other hand, most of us have trouble functioning in the same room with a child (or an adult, for that matter) who is having a tantrum. A better solution is to scoop the angry little child up in your arms, being careful to protect yourself from flailing extremities, and walk the child into her bedroom. If she is still in a crib, put her in it and then leave. Shut the door; latch it if you have to. As you are leaving tell the child that she can come out when she is quiet and ready to behave properly. If your child also bangs her head on the floor (or anything hard, for that matter) when she is angry you might want to pad her crib so that you won't have to worry about her hurting herself. She won't anyway, but the padding will make it easier for you to leave the room.

One advantage of taking your tantruming child to her room is that she may fall asleep and get some much-needed rest. A second is that it puts a bit of a sound buffer between the two of you, and it makes it easier for you to walk away and cool down. In the section about school-age children, I will again discuss tantrums and introduce another management technique. However, common to the management of tantrums in all ages is realization that fatigue is often at the root of the problem and that good sleep management is your best prevention.

Masturbation

Yes, young children do masturbate. It is a behavior that many girls discover even before they can walk. For some reason, boys don't stumble upon it until puberty. However, I know of at least one two-year-old boy who liked to hold his penis when he was tired. It seemed to be his security object.

If your daughter enjoys "riding" her wadded-up blanket or stuffed toy, you don't need to worry that she is being sexually abused. Masturbation is normal, but it may indicate that she is overtired. Many young girls form an association between masturbation and falling asleep, just as some children want to suck their thumbs when they are getting ready to fall asleep.

Even if you don't notice this link between fatigue and your daughter's masturbation, most pediatricians recommend that you tell her to go to her room when she wants to masturbate. Make it clear that she is not being punished. Emphasize that there is a time and a place for everything, and that masturbation is a private thing to be done in her own personal space. You may add that her desire to masturbate may indicate that she is tired and remind her that her bedroom has always been the place to go when she feels tired.

If you are concerned because your daughter continues to masturbate excessively even though she appears to be well rested, you can try to provide her with some extra physical attention. For example, give her more hugs, pats on the head, and cuddles on the couch. This increase in parental touching has been observed to decrease the frequency of masturbatory behavior in small children.

Rocking

In the process of developing sleep independence some children discover that rhythmic body movements help them to relax. As opposed to masturbation, this phenomenon seems to be more of a little boy thing. Of course, this kind of self-stimulatory behavior is observed in some children who have significant developmental delays or who have been neglected and/or abused. However, many normal children will sit and rock when they are tired. I have known several families in whom the behavior seems to have been inherited. It can be quite irritating to everyone else in the home who must listen to the *thump, thump, thumping* until the little rocker drifts off to sleep. It is hard to ignore even if you understand that the behavior does not usually indicate a medical or psychological problem.

If your child is a rocker you should make sure that she is getting enough sleep. You will almost always be able to decrease this annoying behavior dramatically by keeping her well rested. Second, you should do whatever you can to minimize the tactile reward gained from rocking. This may mean adding cross braces to the legs of the crib or even screwing the crib securely to the wall. These may seem like drastic steps, but if the crib won't shake much of the pleasure goes out of the rocking and the behavior will decrease or even disappear.

Tics and Stuttering

Toddlers and preschoolers are still in the process of developing their language skills, and it is not unusual for them to stumble over a word at the beginning of a sentence or phrase. It often seems that their brains have raced out ahead of their little tongues. Stammering or stuttering is to be expected in this age group, and it is impossible to predict which of these children will continue to be stutterers when they are ten years old.

Although most of the time there is no obvious reason for a three-year-old to begin stuttering, I have often observed that these children have more stuttering episodes if they are overtired. Of course, you should also consider the possibility that some anxiety-provoking event has triggered the problem. Forced toilet training, a death in the family, and marital turmoil are just a few of the factors in addition to fatigue that can prompt a child to stumble over words.

Young children are also prone to develop tics such as sniffing, throat clearing, and eye blinking. Just as with stuttering, these repetitive behaviors are often unexplained. However, they seem to be much worse if the child is overtired. The best approach is to ignore the tic and make sure your child is going to bed at a healthy time and getting an appropriate amount of rest. Drawing the child's attention to the behavior often increases her anxiety and aggravates the problem. You should consult your pediatrician if the tic does not subside after a month or two of adequate rest.

Accident-Proneness

After the first few months of life, the largest risk to the health of your child is accidents. Two-year-olds are frequent victims of accidental injury. They are adventuresome and often fearless and have little past experience with the hazards of the new world that their developing mobility is opening around them. Fatigue can frequently be a major contributor to the risk of accidental injury. The child prone to the paradoxical hyperactivity associated with sleep deprivation is much more likely to crash because she is moving at high speed through her environment. Like the rest of us, children tend to lose some of the sharpness of their reflexes as they become more exhausted. Those of us in pediatric practice notice that children with injuries are more likely to roll into the office at times of the day when we would expect their fatigue to be the greatest. Many of the children in my practice who have been labeled "accident-prone" are children with poor sleep habits who are often sleep-deprived.

As your baby grows, a new list of challenges and dilemmas come up. However, they are neither overwhelming nor unmanageable. By remembering that your child's behavior will be adversely affected by sleep deprivation, by following some of the recommendations here, and by keeping close contact with your pediatrician you won't merely survive the twos, you will come to enjoy them.

Is My Child Overtired?

Summary of Strategies

- Work hard to retain your child's naps as long as you can.

- Weld the afternoon nap tightly to your child's lunch.

- Float lunch earlier if your child is acting tired.

- Retain an after-lunch siesta, even after your child has stopped napping completely.

- Develop a safe and effective discipline program that uses time-outs in the child's room.

6

SICK AND TIRED OR JUST PLAIN TIRED?

I suspect that, like most parents, you worry that your child is sick when he complains of being tired. You wonder if he is coming down with an infection or has become anemic—or even worse, whether he could have developed leukemia. Although most illnesses are accompanied by fatigue, there are usually enough other symptoms such as poor appetite and fever to help you zero in on a diagnosis. Sometimes the first and only sign of sickness is lack of energy. However, in a few hours or a few days your child's appearance and complaints will provide ample evidence that he is ill.

On the other hand, if day after day your child tells you that he is tired and no other symptoms develop, the answer is simple. He just isn't getting enough sleep. I guess it is just human nature to ignore the simplest solution first.

At least several times each week I sit down with a family and tell them that after examining their child I can find no other explanation for his fatigue than his lack of sleep. Usually they are relieved to learn that their child is not suffering from a rare tropical disease or a vitamin deficiency. Occasionally I will order a few blood tests or an X ray to help reassure all of us that we can safely get down to the sleep solution by reinstituting naps, creating earlier bedtimes, and trimming overfilled schedules.

Although the most likely cause of your child's fatigue is inadequate sleep, please consult the pediatrician if you have any suspicion that your child may be ill. If you have made all of the recommended adjustments in his sleep schedule and your child is still dragging around, call the doctor again and ask her if she thinks another search for sickness is in order. No one more than I would like to blame all of your child's symptoms on sleep deprivation, but fatigue can be the only sign of significant illness. It doesn't happen often, but don't stop looking for medical causes if your child continues to be tired all of the time.

> *Although inadequate sleep is the most likely cause of your child's fatigue, consult the pediatrician if you suspect that your child may be ill.*

Fatigue in Disguise

While on one hand illness is a major cause of fatigue, sleep deprivation is an often unrecognized contributor to symptoms so dramatic that you may be convinced your child is sick. Unfortunately, few physicians realize how frequently their patients' complaints are the result of inadequate sleep. These associations were certainly not part of my medical school education, but they have become obvious during more than a quarter of a million encounters with patients over the last quarter of a century. Although my busy practice has prevented me from performing carefully controlled scientific experiments, I am convinced by the consistency of my observations that many of my patients' problems are the result of sleep deprivation.

However, before you try to manage your child's leg pains or headaches or vomiting merely by adjusting his bedtime, please go see your pediatrician for a thorough investigation of the problem. Fatigue may not be the only cause of your child's symptoms, and I don't want you to follow me down the garden path away from the correct diagnosis.

If your pediatrician can't find an explanation for your child's complaints, I am sure you can safely try my suggestions for sleep management. Don't be surprised that your child's doctor may not have heard that sleep deprivation can cause leg pains or migraine headaches. She probably hasn't seen it in a textbook, because I haven't either. I hope she will be supportive of your attempts to manage the problem by altering your child's sleep habits.

Remember, don't allow *biologic variation* to fool you into thinking that your child's symptoms couldn't be due to fatigue. Just because your friends' children don't get headaches or leg aches even though they go to bed an hour and a half later doesn't mean that sleep deprivation isn't a cause of your child's symptoms.

I suspect that there are hundreds of illnesses and symptoms that are triggered by sleep deprivation. However, in this chapter I will discuss just a few in which the association has been most obvious to me.

Growing Pains

Thirty-five or forty years ago, physicians would often tell parents that a child's leg discomfort was the result of "growing pains." As we swing into the new millennium most well-educated pediatricians have learned that normal growth should be a painless process, and so the diagnosis of growing pains has fallen into disuse. Unfortunately, grandmothers, aunts, and the next-door neighbor are more than willing to resurrect this old label whenever a child complains that his legs hurt.

However, there does seem to be a rather poorly defined collection of symptoms that I refer to as "nocturnal leg pains of childhood," and it is probably what many doctors were talking about when they referred to growing pains. The child's discomfort is primarily in the muscles of the lower leg, but it could involve the thighs or feet. The pain does not occur in the ankles or knees. In fact, if your child is complaining of predominantly joint pain he probably has some other problem, and you should consult the pediatrician.

The discomfort can come late in the afternoon or wake your

child out of a sound sleep in the middle of the night. It may affect one leg or both. The pain can be very intense and does not respond to medication. Occasionally, your child may ask to have his legs rubbed. The episode may last for just a few minutes or an hour. By morning there is no lingering discomfort.

To my knowledge no one has discovered the biochemical process behind this painful phenomenon. However, fatigue can trigger it. I am not talking about overuse. Running or jumping to excess can cause muscle soreness in older children and adolescents that will usually persist into the daytime. On the other hand, most young children can run all day long without discomfort. The pains I am referring to are caused by sleep deprivation, not an excess of activity.

For example, you plan a family trip to the circus. The night before, your child sleeps poorly because he is anticipating an exciting day. He gets up early, enjoys the circus, and goes to bed late because you stop at a restaurant on the way home. He actually was less physically active than usual because he was sitting most of the day. However, he wakes at 1:00 A.M. with terrible calf pain and asks you to rub his legs until he falls asleep half an hour later. The next morning he sleeps an hour later more than usual and wakes with his legs feeling fine.

Sometimes the cause of the fatigue is not as obvious as a trip to the circus. The sleep deprivation may accumulate over several days until one night the child awakens with leg pains. Occasionally, I can uncover a pattern of sleep deprivation by asking parents if their child's nocturnal leg pains were more likely to occur on any night of the week. For example, I can remember one seven-year-old who usually had leg aches on Wednesday nights. It turns out that Wednesday afternoon was the time he had his Cub Scout meeting and his mother had an aerobics class. The little rest period he usually enjoyed immediately after school was replaced by the hubbub of Cub Scouts, and his mother's aerobics class forced a later dinner and an even later bedtime.

The solution to this seven-year-old's leg pains was simple enough. I encouraged his mother to prepare a dinner earlier in the day that could be warmed up quickly in the microwave as soon as everyone got home. This allowed her little Cub Scout to get to bed closer to his usual bedtime and his leg pains disappeared.

Sometimes nocturnal leg pains cannot be prevented. The circus trip might be an example of such a situation. You could try to keep such a trip a secret until the last moment in the hope of improving the chances that your child will sleep well the night before. It is also important to keep your child as well rested every day as you possibly can. By doing so you can hope that he will have a reserve supply of stamina that will allow him to tolerate the occasional day when he will experience some unavoidable sleep deprivation.

If your child suffers from nocturnal leg pains, it may be difficult for you to imagine that pain of such intensity could be the result of simply not getting enough rest. Try improving your child's sleep patterns. If that doesn't dramatically decrease the frequency of the pain, give your pediatrician another call. You may be dealing with a more serious problem.

Headaches

Headaches can be caused by a wide variety of conditions from brain tumors to viral infections. Although you may think that headaches are relatively uncommon in young children, they actually occur rather frequently in this age group. Because they may be occasionally associated with some very worrisome illnesses, your first stop should be at the pediatrician's office. After a thorough examination, including a blood pressure measurement, the doctor should be able to reassure you that nothing serious is going on. She may also suggest a trip to the ophthalmologist or optometrist just to make sure that your child's vision has not deteriorated since his last exam.

If your child is not obviously ill and has passed the pediatrician's exam, then the cause of his headaches is probably . . . you guessed it . . . fatigue. I have seen it happen, year after year, patient after patient, for more than twenty-five years. Sometimes the headaches can be so intense that they make the child vomit, but the answer is still a very simple one: more sleep.

Fatigue-related headaches usually do not occur before late morning. In fact, if your child is having early-morning headaches, particularly if they are associated with vomiting, he should see a neurologist to rule out more serious conditions. Typically, the sleep-deprived child will have headaches in late afternoon or early evening, but they can occur at any time of day. The child may look pale and ask to lie down in a dark room.

> *Fatigue-related headaches usually do not occur before late morning.*

The headache may be in any part of his head and may be described as sharp or dull, pounding or squeezing. The pain may not be very severe, but it can be very intense and last for fifteen minutes or several hours. If the child begins to vomit, this usually signals that the headache will be ending soon. The child may then fall into a deep sleep for half an hour or many hours. He will then awaken pain free. Medication is usually not very helpful, primarily because the child can't hold down the medicine.

Most physicians would probably label the more severe fatigue headaches as migraines. I prefer to be more specific and call them "childhood migraines," because they usually lack some of the signs more typical of adult migraines, such as visual disturbances and numbness of one side of the body. However, older children and adolescents may experience these symptoms. I am not sure whether children with these fatigue-related headaches go on to have migraines as adults, because most of my patients seem to improve once they discover that they can avoid headaches by getting more sleep.

You may have observed already that when your child is tired he is more likely to develop a headache. However, childhood migraines can be so intense and dramatic that it may be difficult for you to believe pain that severe can be triggered simply by lack of sleep. It is particularly hard to accept if the headache comes on suddenly and without warning, as it may. However, most children who are coming down with a fatigue headache will begin to look tired and a little pale before the pain actually begins.

Unfortunately, by the time these warning signs appear, it is usually too late to do anything about the situation. However, if your child has not begun to vomit, it is worth trying to give ibuprofen or acetaminophen at this early stage. But don't be surprised if it has no effect because the process is too far advanced to respond. Ushering your child to a dark room and having him lie down is about all you can do until the episode passes.

Prevention is really the only answer, and of course this can be rather complex and difficult to achieve. If you can see an obvious correlation between certain activities such as sleep-overs or late nights watching television, make the obvious changes in your child's social calendar to avoid these situations. It is cruel and unproductive to dredge up the old I-told-you-so routine while your child is in pain. However, the next day you should point out to him the association between his late night and the headache.

If your child is having more than one or two headaches per month and you are unable to see any specific events that are creating the fatigue, chronic sleep deprivation is the problem. In other words, day in and day out your child is just not getting quite enough sleep. The condition may be so mild that there are no obvious symptoms. However, in this overtired state it takes only a little more activity, such as a close soccer game or an extra-busy day at school, to drain his stamina tank dry and push him over the brink to a severe headache.

When you are faced with these chronic situations, you must step back and look at your entire family schedule to find a solution. It will probably involve an earlier bedtime and/or reinstitution of a nap for the younger child. This may require a change in mealtimes and work schedules, and a reassessment of number, timing, and importance of after-school activities.

Although I would like to promise that if you follow all my advice about sleep and schedules your child will no longer have any headaches, I think that is an unrealistic goal. Some children are so vulnerable to fatigue that it doesn't take much sleep deprivation to trigger a headache. While I am sure you will be able to decrease the number of your child's headaches with good sleep management, I am equally sure that you won't be able to completely eliminate them. Please don't take these as discouraging words. If your child is having fatigue-related headaches I am confident you will be pleased with the improvement you will achieve by improving his sleep habits. However, remember that if the headaches are not getting better you should consult the pediatrician again. Please give her another chance to look for a more serious problem.

Bellyaches and Vomiting

If your child complains of a bellyache and begins to vomit he probably has "stomach flu"—or more correctly, gastroenteritis. However, there are nearly a dozen organs and more than thirty feet of intestines hidden inside his abdominal cavity, and there are thousands of illnesses and malfunctions that can provoke pain and vomiting. Although it should be down near the bottom, fatigue deserves a place on the long list of causes of bellyaches. As you have just read, childhood migraines may be associated with vomiting, and occasionally the abdominal pain and vomiting overshadow the headache. There is one very frustrating condition, sometimes known as "cyclic vomiting," in which the unfortunate child is plagued by long bouts of vomiting and discomfort for which no other obvious cause can be found. These episodes may come as infrequently as once or twice a year or as often as once a week. It seems to me that this problem should probably be considered a close cousin of childhood migraine and as such may have some relationship to sleep deprivation. However, the bottom line is if your child experiences abdominal pain and/or vomiting on a regular basis, your first stop should be at the pediatrician's. Don't be surprised if she suggests numerous blood tests and X rays, and be even less surprised if they are all normal. This doesn't mean that you were wasting your time. Abdominal pain can be the symptom of some very serious diseases.

On the other hand, while you are pursuing a thorough investigation of the problem try to implement some of the suggestions in Chapters 5 and 8. You might find that when your child is more rested the episodes of abdominal pain disappear.

Bedwetting

About 18 percent of four-year-olds and nearly 11 percent of six-year-olds wet their beds, although many have been daytime toilet trained for many years. At least half of the children who are currently bedwetters will achieve night dryness in the next twelve months. As long as your child is not having daytime accidents or experiencing urinary tract infections or other voiding problems, nocturnal enuresis (bedwetting) should be considered a normal, but frustrating, phenomenon that he will outgrow.

> *In most cases bedwetting is a sleep-related problem that will be outgrown.*

Most bedwetters are very deep sleepers and seem oblivious to the soggy sheets that surround them. If you attempt to wake your bedwetter before you go to bed you may find it impossible. If you succeed, he will probably not fully awaken and must be led like a zombie to the bathroom.

Because bedwetting is a sleep-related phenomenon, it will not resolve until your child develops more mature sleep patterns and a larger bladder capacity. There is little you can do to speed along the process of resolution before age six or seven, and you will have little success until your child is committed to solving the problem. This is not to say that your child is bedwetting because he doesn't care, it is merely an observation that children are unlikely to respond to treatments until they want to be a part of the solution.

In fact, I have observed that if parents try to force a "cure" before their bedwetter is ready they are likely to pay the price of having a poorly rested child. For example, you may have been advised to take your child to the bathroom at your bedtime. Occasionally, this tactic may keep him dry for the night, but by interrupting his sleep patterns you may be perpetuating his tendency to sleep so deeply that his brain doesn't respond to the cries for help emanating from his bladder. Even worse, by waking him at night you may be depriving him of enough sleep to create an unpleasant and unhealthy fatigue situation the next day.

The same caution goes for the electronic "bed buzzers" or "wee alarms." These gadgets are safe and can be effective in hustling along a resolution of enuresis by waking the child when moisture reaches the sensor in his underpants. Many pediatricians recommend them to families of bedwetters. However, if your child is not approaching his natural cure of the problem, the buzz of the alarm can disrupt his sleep so severely that you end up trading a well-rested bedwetter for an exhausted child and dry bedclothes.

Please don't let me discourage you from trying these gadgets if your child is begging you for help with his bedwetting. Warn your child that they may not wake him if he is sleeping too soundly, and be alert to the trade-off between an occasional dry bed and an overtired child.

If your child is wetting the bed every night, you will probably not notice any correlation between fatigue and bedwetting, although it may exist. As he gets to the point where he is only wetting several nights each week, you may notice that if your child has had a busy day or gone to bed late he is more likely to wet. Of course, this makes sense. The more tired he is, the more likely it is that he will sleep so deeply that his bladder's cries for help go unheeded, and he will wet the bed.

When your child gets to the stage when an association between his sleep schedule and bedwetting is obvious, you can and should point this out to him. He may be motivated enough to go along with your suggestions about earlier bedtimes and more carefully scheduled days in the hope of avoiding the discomfort and embarrassment of waking up in the morning in a soggy bed.

If your child is wetting every night it is certainly worth taking a hard look at his total sleep time, the demands of his daytime schedule, and evidence of other signs of fatigue. Try to create more opportunities for sleep and rest and see if he begins to have a few dry nights. If he does, a cure is in sight.

Rest or Ritalin? Which Does Your Child Need?

Attention Deficit Disorders (ADD) with and without hyperactivity have become hot topics over the last decade. It seems as though every classroom has at least one child taking Ritalin to help him stay on task. Despite all the interest in the subject, scientists still have not been able to provide physicians and psychologists with the tools necessary to diagnose ADD with certainty.

No one seems to understand why there are so many children in this country who appear distractible and/or hyperactive, and why many of them appear to improve when they are given stimulant medication. Is it a genetic thing? We know that many children with symptoms of ADD have family members with similar problems. Have parents and school systems become so permissive that the society allows these behaviors to flourish? Could some as-yet-unidentified environmental toxin be to blame? Could it be dietary? Recent studies have shown that despite what you may have been told, sugar is *not* a contributor to hyperactivity.

The problem certainly isn't imaginary. There do seem to be many more distractible and hyperactive children than there were twenty years ago, and some of them become more focused when they are given stimulant medication.

One explanation for this phenomenon involves sleep deprivation. In Chapter 5 I introduced the concept of paradoxical hyperactivity, which causes many toddlers to spin like little dervishes when they are overtired. I am sure that a similar relationship between fatigue and hyperactivity occurs in some older children and adults as well. In fact, I have recently read reports by other physicians and psychologists whose observations have lead them to suspect an association between sleep deprivation and short attention span and impulsive behavior.

This may be one explanation for why Ritalin is effective in treating Attention Deficit Disorders. If your child is distractible or hyperactive because he hasn't gotten enough sleep, Ritalin may help him pay attention simply because it wakes him up. We may be using large quantities of stimulant medication in this country because we have so many sleep-deprived children.

On one hand, some children who are hyperactive and distractible may have a specific structural or biochemical problem in their brains that for some as-yet-undiscovered reason responds to Ritalin. On the other hand, there are thousands of other children who appear distractible and hyperactive not because there is something a little unusual about their brain chemistry but just because they are overtired. Many of these fatigued children will seem to improve on stimulant medication simply because the drug helps them to stay more awake.

Although not every child with symptoms of distractibility and hyperactivity will be dramatically cured by a good night's sleep, you have nothing to lose by putting some effort into fatigue prevention. At a minimum it will help your child be less distractible and less hyperactive.

> *If you believe that your child has ADD you have nothing to lose by including fatigue management in your behavior management plan.*

If you suspect that your child may have ADD or ADHD (attention deficit with hyperactivity), begin with a visit to your pediatrician and/or a child psychologist. They will probably initiate a series of tests, examinations, and observations to define your child's learning abilities and disabilities. Simultaneously, take an inventory of your child's sleep habits and sleep needs. Follow the suggestions in Chapters 5 and 8 as you attempt to create a schedule that will allow your child to become well rested. You may be pleasantly surprised to find that your child's distractibility and hyperactivity are diminished, and maybe that they even disappear. I have seen scores of children who had been diagnosed with ADD who were "cured" by good sleep management. You will not have wasted your time even if your child is eventually diagnosed as having ADD or ADHD. He will be much easier to manage if he is getting enough sleep. Children with ADD have good days and bad days just like the rest of us, and our bad days tend to occur when we are overtired. By keeping your child with ADD from becoming sleep deprived you and he and his teachers will have many more good days.

Summary of Strategies

- Although the most likely cause for your child's fatigue is inadequate sleep, consult the pediatrician to rule out illness.

- If your child is having late-afternoon headaches or muscular leg pains at night, sleep deprivation is the most likely cause.

- If your child is wetting his bed only one or two nights per week, you may be able to solve the problem by seeing that he gets more sleep.

- If your child is impulsive and seems to have a short attention span, some of his behavior may improve if he is given an earlier bedtime.

7

BUMPS IN THE NIGHT

As you learned in Chapter 3, children often wake in the middle of the night for no obvious reason. Unfortunately, many of them must be reminded that it is their job and not yours to put themselves back to sleep. There are also a handful of nocturnal disruptions that may not be associated with a complete awakening. Some of these can be quite alarming and others may have important health implications.

Nightmares

A dream suddenly turns ugly and the train is going to run over us, or a Tyrannosaurus rex has just tossed our playmate over his shoulder and now he is after us. When your child is having a nightmare she will be obviously awake when you find her. She will be able to tell you what she was dreaming about, and in the morning she will remember the event.

Although nightmares and bad dreams can indicate that something is troubling your child, most of the time they are not trying to tell us something ominous about her psyche. They seem to be more common if your child is overtired, but I haven't been impressed that the association is very strong.

> *Nightmares and bad dreams are not usually a warning sign that your child is having serious psychological problems.*

When your child wakes you to tell you about her nightmare, your first response should be to calm her down and reassure her that it was only a bad dream. However, resist the temptation to turn on the lights and take her downstairs for a snack. Sometimes "bad dreams" can become an excuse to go sleep with Mommy and Daddy or go down to the living room for a video. Try to confine the scenario to her bedroom so that bad habits and associations don't develop.

If you observe a dramatic increase in the number of your child's nightmares or the subject matter is falling into a pattern, you should sit down and think about what could be triggering these bad dreams. Is there trouble at school? Trouble with friends? A death in the family or neighborhood (don't forget pets)? Marital discord? Ask for the assistance of your pediatrician, a child psychologist, or a psychiatrist.

Violent TV shows and videos can often trigger bad dreams. Sometimes the subject matter may not seem frightening to you, but for some reason your child may find it very upsetting. This is just one more reason to keep tabs on your child's viewing menu.

Night Terrors

Night terrors are often mistaken for nightmares, but their management is quite different. The usual scenario begins with you being wakened at two in the morning by what sound like cries for help. You rush into her room and find her sitting up in bed, eyes open, screaming about something, but you can't quite make out all of the words. You attempt to comfort her, but she fights you off. You try to communicate with her, but she doesn't respond appropriately. It is as though she doesn't see you. Eventually she either falls back to sleep or you succeed in waking her, but she can't tell you what was bothering her. In the morning she doesn't recall the event except that you woke her.

As you can imagine, these arousals are very frightening if you are a parent witnessing one for the first time. You might worry that they are the result of some psychological trauma of which you are unaware, or you might be concerned that your child is suffering in pain. Neither of these is the case. Night terrors are very common, so common that they might even be considered normal. They do not indicate that your child has suppressed some sinister event that has occurred at day care. Your child doesn't even know that they are occurring. Night terrors may be painful for us to watch, but they aren't bothering your child—although this may be hard to believe as you watch her shriek and thrash about.

Like sleepwalking, the other common arousal phenomenon, they occur much more frequently when children are overtired. Most sleep experts suggest that you resist your natural urge to interrupt them, because waking your child can aggravate the sleep deprivation that may have caused the terror in the first place. If you succeed in getting your child to wake from her night terror, you will disrupt her sleep pattern and may find yourself faced with the challenge of getting her back to sleep. Of course, it is hard to stand back and watch your child, wide-eyed and shrieking in apparent terror. However, your role is to make sure that she is in a safe environment and can't injure herself. Try your hardest to avoid waking her.

> *Resist the natural urge to wake your child when she is having a night terror, because interrupting her sleep may aggravate the sleep deprivation that has triggered the terror.*

If your child is having frequent night terrors (more than once or twice a month), you should take a hard look at her sleep schedule. An earlier bedtime, a return to the after-lunch siesta, and a less-hectic daytime routine may be in order.

Sleepwalking

Sleepwalking is more akin to night terrors than nightmares. Your child might initially seem awake, eyes open, maybe even be mumbling something or ambulating purposefully but not appropriately. A common scenario finds the sleepwalking child urinating in his wastebasket or closet instead of the toilet.

Tales about sleepwalkers can be very amusing. However, sleepwalking can be dangerous. Open windows, balconies, kitchens, bathrooms, stairways, and busy streets are just some of the hazards that await the somnambulist. If your child is a sleepwalker you must do everything you can think of to protect her from the environment. Put a gate across her doorway, latch her door, put a bell on the door to alert you when she is roaming. These are just a few examples of steps you may have to take to keep her safe.

In my experience the tendency to sleepwalk appears to be inherited. Obviously it is too late to do anything about that. However, sleepwalking occurs more frequently when a child is sleep-deprived. This is a factor you can control by establishing earlier bedtimes and reinstituting naps. Keep this in mind, because in addition to going to the hardware store for latches and bells, you should work on getting your sleepwalker more rest.

More Not-So-Silent Nights

Most of the sleep-deprived children in my practice have gotten that way as the result of poor scheduling and/or ineffective behavior management. However, there are some medical problems that can contribute to sleep deprivation. These conditions may shorten your child's total amount of sleep by causing her to wake frequently, but they may also affect the quality of her sleep without causing her to become fully awake. As you can imagine, this latter situation might go on for many years undetected. In other words, if your child's sleep is merely disturbed but not completely interrupted she may not be awake enough to alert you to the problem.

Sleep Apnea

"Sleep apnea," sometimes known as obstructive sleep apnea, is a good example of a situation in which your child's sleep is inadequate in quality but you may never be aware of the problem because she never becomes fully awake. Here is how it can happen. When your child lies down and goes to sleep, gravity and the natural relaxation of the muscles and tissues in her head and neck can dramatically alter the size and shape of the air passages that lead into her windpipe. This is particularly true if your child has very large adenoids (the tonsil-like tissue located at the back of the nasal passages). These collections of lymph tissue may interfere with her breathing a bit when she is awake, and she may sound a bit "nasal," but over time she has learned to breathe through her mouth to compensate for this obstruction. However, when she goes to sleep and the tissues around her head and neck relax, your child's already narrowed breathing passages may become so small that she is unable to get enough air into her lungs.

Fortunately, our bodies have sensors that can detect this unhealthy situation and send an appropriate message to our brain that says, "Hey! Wake up and breathe better, we've got an oxygen problem here!" Sometimes this results in a full awakening, but it is more likely that your child will arouse just enough to take a bigger breath or to change the position of her body to relieve the constriction. Once the air flow is improved she will gradually slip back into a deeper sleep until the airway-narrowing situation becomes critical again and another arousal occurs. The process continues to cycle through the night. You can imagine that a sleep pattern that is frequently interrupted by a recurring airway obstruction is not very restful. If your child's body must spend several hours at night in a partially awake state just so that she can breathe, you can expect her to be tired, cranky, and distractible during the day.

There are numerous causes of upper airway obstruction. Some children are born with large adenoids or tonsils. These lymph tissues may become swollen because of infection or allergy. Less frequently, the airway narrowing occurs as the result of a deformity in the child's nose or windpipe.

Obesity can also aggravate nocturnal breathing problems. When an overweight child lies down her breathing muscles must work harder to move her chest simply because it weighs more. Imagine how it would feel if you had thirty-five pounds of lead sitting on your chest. To make matters worse, fat accumulated around the tissues of her head and neck can contribute to further airway narrowing.

The symptoms of nocturnal upper airway obstruction can sometimes be difficult to interpret. Snoring can be a clue that your child is having trouble breathing at night. However, most children who snore do not have sleep apnea. Many children snore when their upper airways are relaxed or slightly swollen by a cold. Even if your child snores loudly she probably doesn't have significant airway obstruction. On the other hand, if there are occasional long pauses between her inspirations this may indicate a problem. If it sounds as though your child is struggling to get her breath or if she must sleep with her head tipped back, sleep apnea should be considered.

> *Although snoring can be a clue that your child is having trouble breathing, most children who snore do not have sleep apnea.*

The first stop should be at your pediatrician's office for a thorough exam. Before you call for an appointment, I suggest that you attempt to make an audiotape of your child's snoring. If you have a video camera that will work in low light, a videotape would be even better. Bring the tape along with you to the doctor visit. It is very helpful if you can edit the tape or set it up in the tape machine so that the pediatrician can take it home and review the most dramatic segments without having to listen for an hour.

Your child's doctor may not be interested in such a recording, but I have found that I have been able to reassure many parents that their children's nocturnal breathing patterns were normal on the basis of a routine physical examination and a homemade audiotape or videotape.

If the pediatrician suspects that your child might be having obstructive airway-related sleep problems, she may do one of several things. She may refer you to an ear, nose, and throat specialist, who may order some head and neck X rays after she has examined your child. She may suggest surgical removal of the enlarged adenoids and/or tonsils. Although this kind of operation is not as complex as open-heart surgery, there are risks, and you may want to get a second opinion before you proceed any further.

If the situation is less obvious your pediatrician may send you to a sleep laboratory for an evaluation. A sleep study involves hooking up your child to numerous sensors that will monitor heart rate, breathing, brain waves, and the oxygen content of her blood, to name just a few tests. All these parameters are measured and a video recording is made while your child is asleep. These studies can be expensive and are usually not undertaken when a child has obviously enlarged adenoids or tonsils. If your child is obese or if the cause of her excessive daytime drowsiness is un-clear, the study may be more helpful.

If the doctor suspects that an allergy may be contributing to the airway narrowing, she might prescribe medication or consult an allergist. However, if attempts to get the allergies under con-trol after several months are not completely successful a visit to the ENT specialist would be appropriate.

There are many children who exhibit very loud snoring and even some long inspiratory pauses when they have a cold or dur-ing the worst of their allergic season. As long as these periods of relative airway obstruction last only a few weeks at a time, I would not be terribly concerned. On the other hand, if your child consistently exhibits signs of fatigue, is overweight, and/or is a noisy breather at night, please give the pediatrician a call.

Ear Infections

Earaches are a common cause of interrupted sleep for children, their parents, and their doctors. Exactly why they seem to occur more often at night is unknown. If your child is old enough to ac-tually tell you that she has an earache the situation is straightfor-ward. You can try to make her more comfortable by propping her up and giving her a pain medication such as acetaminophen or ibuprofen. A warm water bottle or a heating pad on the painful ear might help, but the most intense discomfort will probably be gone by morning regardless of what you do. In fact, the pain may have disappeared and your child may not even remember which ear was hurting. Nonetheless, give the pediatrician a call in the morning for an evaluation and possible treatment.

If your child is too young to speak, the cause of your child's interrupted sleep may not be so obvious. Ear infections are usually associated with upper respiratory infections (colds) and are usually accompanied by a fever, but there are plenty of exceptions. If you have been successful in helping your child develop good sleep habits, a night of disturbed sleep will stick out like a sore thumb. You may not know whether the cause is an ear infection or a stomachache, but you will be aware that something is wrong. If, on the other hand, your child is an erratic sleeper, you may find yourself making more than the average number of false alarm visits to the doctor. Were last night's wake-ups just her usual bad night, or was she in pain? It can be very difficult to be sure. This is just one more good reason to focus your efforts on keeping your child well-rested.

Although it is easy to imagine why the pain of an acute ear infection would wake your child, a collection of uninfected fluid behind her eardrum may also interfere with her sleep. Fluid often accumulates in your child's middle ear when she has a cold or is recuperating from an ear infection. She may perceive it as a bubbly or popping sensation. If she is old enough to speak she may mention that her ear feels plugged. Although the symptoms that can accompany middle ear fluid aren't intense enough to be described as pain, they often seem to interfere with a child's sleep patterns.

In the last few years the medical management of these fluid collections has undergone several changes. You should discuss the treatment, and nontreatment, options with your pediatrician.

Pinworms

I was taught in medical school that between 30 and 40 percent of small children had pinworms. Fortunately, most of these children and their parents were unaware that they were hosting these little (one-quarter to one-half-inch-long) white, threadlike wigglers, because pinworms usually don't cause dramatic symptoms. They spend most of their life cycle in the child's rectum. However, at night they migrate out onto the skin just an inch or less from the rectal opening. Once in the outside world they lay microscopic eggs and then return to the warmth of the rectum.

This migration and egg laying could cause an itchy sensation and wake the child. However, most of the time children sleep through the event. When the child scratches her bottom the microscopic eggs can end up on her fingers. When she puts her fingers in her mouth the eggs find their way into her GI tract and eventually hatch in her rectum to keep the cycle going. The invisible eggs may also be passed to a playmate who will likewise give them a warm place to grow when she sucks her thumb or chews on her fingernails.

If your child is having unexplained night wakings, particularly if she is also having rectal itching, check for pinworms. This can be done by inspecting the area around her rectum with a flashlight after she has been asleep for fifteen or twenty minutes. If you find live worms, don't freak out. She has had them for weeks before you discovered them, and they don't cause any medical problem other than the itching. It can wait until morning, when you can call the pediatrician for some medication.

Rarely, a pinworm will get disoriented after it has laid its eggs and will find its way into a little girl's vagina. When this occurs, the discomfort can be quite intense. There really isn't much to be done, except giving the unfortunate child a warm bath. The worm can't survive in that location, and the situation usually doesn't last more than an hour or so.

There are other causes of nocturnal rectal itching, including food allergies and infections. The search for a culprit can be frustrating. Until one is found, a warm bath and some hydrocortisone cream may help.

Eczema and Other Itchy Skin Conditions

Dermatologists are just beginning to explore the relationship between sleep and a collection of itchy skin rashes of which eczema (also known as "atopic dermatitis") is the best known. Many children with eczema complain that itching keeps them awake at night. However, the researchers have discovered that sleep deprivation may contribute to the itching. This is just another unfortunate example of the poor getting poorer. It doesn't seem fair. Your child's itching keeps her awake, and she loses several hours of sleep. The resulting sleep deprivation makes her itch more, and the process just keeps going around and around in a vicious cycle. To make matters worse, some scientists have even suggested that the growth hormone production lost as the result of sleep deprivation may explain why children with atopic dermatitis often do not grow as tall as expected.

Some dermatologists suggest that one of the most important sleep management techniques you should employ is to keep the bedroom cool. In addition to its general sleep benefit it may prevent sweating, which can aggravate your child's natural tendency to scratch. The bottom line is that if your child is troubled by an itchy skin condition such as eczema, seborrhea, or hives, you should try all of the techniques outlined in this book to keep her well rested. It may help her skin much more than you might have guessed.

Getting Back on Schedule After the Illness Is Over

We expect children to wake at night when they are sick. Earaches, plugged noses, and itchy rashes are bound to interrupt sleep. The problem is that many children don't return to their usual healthy sleep patterns promptly when the worst of an illness has passed. For example, your three-year-old has had a cold for four or five days, her sleep has been a little erratic, but one night she has a terrible time and seems to be in pain. The next day the pediatrician finds an ear infection and prescribes some antibiotics. Your child wakes three times the night after you start the medication, which isn't too surprising, but she continues to wake once or twice each night even though her temperature is gone and her nasal congestion seems much improved. What should you do? Is it safe or humane to let her cry herself back to sleep again?

In the scenario I have described, you can begin to apply the Ferberization or cold-turkey strategies to help your recuperating child relearn how to put herself to sleep. Usually, by the second night after the start of antibiotics, most if not all of the ear pain is gone, and you can allow your child to cry without feeling guilty about it. However, you should consult the pediatrician if your child continues to sleep erratically after the worst of her illness has appeared to pass. Most of the time your hunch will be correct and the pediatrician will give you the go-ahead to reinstitute the sleep rules you have implemented previously—although she may want to reexamine your child before she says it is okay to let her cry. Don't be afraid to ask for help, but don't delay. Many parents wait too long to resume the old rules after an illness has subsided. Your child doesn't have to be completely well to put herself back to sleep.

> *When your child is ill give her the attention she needs in her own bed, not yours.*

After an illness, you can make this transition back to business as usual easier by being careful to bend as few rules as possible when your child is sick. Don't bring her into bed with you. When you comfort her, do it in her room. If she wants to be out of her bed, rock her in a chair. If she wants a drink, bring it to her room. Bad habits that develop during an illness can be hard to break. The less you stray from her usual routines, the less you will have to rebuild when the illness is over.

Summary of Strategies

- Resist the temptation to wake your child if she is having a night terror.

- If your child is having frequent night terrors or episodes of sleepwalking, she might be sleep-deprived.

- If your child is a sleepwalker, make sure that stairways are blocked and unsafe areas are secured.

- If you suspect that your child's snoring is a symptom of sleep apnea, make a video or audiotape and present it to her pediatrician.

- When your child is ill give her the attention she needs in her own room. Don't bring her into bed with you.

8

KEEPING THE SLEEP TRAIN ON THE TRACKS

Even a Well-Rested Child Can Have Sleep Problems

I wish I could guarantee that if you read this book from cover to cover and follow all of my suggestions your child will always sleep well, but I can't. Even children whose parents have been careful to give fatigue prevention a high priority experience sleep problems from time to time.

Illness, travel, and changes in family routines are just a few of the things that can disrupt the sleep patterns of your well-rested child. Fortunately, there are effective techniques for getting him back on track. On the other hand, your child may have developed some bad sleep habits by the time you discovered this book. It's not too late. Even though you may not have taught him sleep independence as an infant, that is water over the dam. You can still help him learn to put himself to sleep at an appropriate time and in an appropriate place. This how-to-fix-it chapter will show you how to get your child to stay in his room at bedtime and what to do when he wakes in the middle of the night or decides to start his day an hour before the rest of the family.

Sleep Refusal

Let's start with the most troublesome problem, sleep refusal. Although you may have established an effective and efficient bedtime ritual even before your child could walk, he may suddenly decide one day that he doesn't want to sleep in his room at a time you know is appropriate. He may claim that he is afraid to be alone in his room. The fear may be the result of a violent television show or it may have no apparent cause. Young children often develop fears without obvious provocation.

He may have become accustomed to staying up an hour or two later while he was visiting Grandma and now doesn't want to miss any action by going to bed at his usual time. More often than not, the abrupt development of sleep refusal is unexplained. It just happens.

First, make sure your child's bedtime is still appropriate. Use the chart on page 18 to help you decide if you are expecting him to get more sleep than a child his age needs. It is likely that his total sleep time is adequate but his afternoon nap may be starting too late. When bedtime comes along he could be too well rested to fall asleep promptly. Reread the portion of Chapter 4 that deals with naps and their timing.

On the other hand your child may be sufficiently tired in the evening but his pre-bedtime ritual may have become too stimulating. Wrestling with Dad or siblings, exciting games, or TV shows may be revving him up so much that he just can't wind down enough to accept the concept of sleep. Obviously, the solution is to replace these activities with more relaxed ones. If you have been away at work all day this change can be difficult to accept, but remember that your child's sleep should get top priority. Save your roughhousing and active play for mornings and weekends.

If your child complains of being afraid of monsters or ghosts, don't spend much time in a rational discussion about why there are no such things, or at least that there aren't any of them in his bedroom. The more detailed your explanation becomes the more your child may become convinced that they exist and are something to be feared. Acknowledge his fears and get on with fixing the problem.

If he wants a *small* night-light, provide one. However, sometimes these lights cast shadows that are frightening. Well before bedtime, sit down and remind him what elements you have both agreed will be part of his bedtime ritual. Consider writing them down or drawing pictograms (see page 71 in Chapter 4 for an example).

Make it clear that the only place your child will be allowed to fall asleep is in his bedroom, not in or on your bed, not on the couch in the family room. Agree that initially you will stay with him in his room until he falls asleep. However, tell him that this is just the first step in a gradual, but steady, weaning process that in a couple of weeks will end with him falling asleep with you outside his room.

> *Make it clear that the <u>only</u> place your child will be allowed to fall asleep is in his bed, not in or on your bed, not on the couch in the family room.*

You can start by sitting (not lying) on your child's bed until he falls asleep. After two nights of this move to a chair next to his bed for two nights, and then every two nights move the chair a couple of feet closer to the door until finally you are sitting outside his bedroom. After two nights of this you can go about your business after you have tucked him in.

This weaning process can be time-consuming, but it is usually effective. Make a rule that you will stay in his bedroom until he falls asleep only once each night. If he wakes a few minutes after you have left the room there is no second chance. This is a situation in which you need to use a tough-love approach that many parents find difficult to accept. However, if you waver and fail to keep your promises/threats, it may take months or even years for a healthy bedtime to be reestablished (or established, if you have never set one before).

If your child comes out of his room or asks you to return, you must refuse and remind him that he has had his bedtime ritual for the night and that now he can put himself to sleep. If necessary, you may need to put up a gate to keep him in his room. Of course, this won't work if your child is old enough to climb over the gate. You can manage his fussing or screaming in one of two ways. You can immediately place him back in his bed, leave the room promptly, and then return after increasingly long intervals of time and repeat the process until he falls asleep. This, of course, is Ferberization. On the other hand, you can allow him to cry himself to sleep without returning. This cold-turkey approach may be a bit more efficient, but you must be able to accept the fact that it is safe and humane to allow your preschooler to fall asleep on the floor by the gate. This can be difficult, but it won't be very many nights before he opts for staying in his bed.

If your child is older you can threaten to turn off his night-light and close his bedroom door if he comes out or keeps calling for unnecessary assistance. For this to be effective you must follow through with your threat. However, the first time you do it, I suggest that you allow your child to wait in the darkness for no longer than thirty seconds to let him know that you mean business. This is usually all that is necessary, but you may need to purchase a latch for the door if he keeps coming out. Many parents have trouble taking this step because they are concerned about its safety, or they are worried about what their friends and neighbors might think. After suggesting this method for more than twenty-five years, I have found it to be both safe and effective. If you are getting tired of trotting your child back to his room, a hook and eye that you can buy at the hardware store for two dollars can solve your problem in a wink. You will probably have to use it only once or twice, but it will continue to hang there as a reminder that you are a parent who keeps her word.

If your child keeps asking for things to extend and delay the bedtime ritual, you must have a plan for dealing with these requests and learn quickly where to draw the line. When thirst is the complaint, leave no more than six ounces of water in a cup or glass in the room as part of the bedtime ritual. When a trip to the toilet is the excuse, leave a potty or the modern equivalent of a chamberpot in the child's room. If he says he is hungry, a firm "No, you will have plenty to eat tomorrow" should be your response. Your child is not going to starve to death overnight He is just using hunger as a ploy to delay his bedtime.

While you are working to remedy your child's sleep refusal he may continue to want to sleep later in the morning. Don't allow this to happen because it will delay the process of resetting his biologic clock. For a few days you may be forced to endure a child who is overtired during the day, but waking him in the morning will help you achieve your ultimate goal of an earlier and more pleasant bedtime more quickly.

You will succeed at managing your child's sleep refusal if you are consistent and persistent. You must continue to remind yourself that keeping your child well rested should be near the top of your priority list. The time and energy you spend helping your child accept a healthy bedtime will be repaid many times over.

Night Wakings

Managing your child's middle-of-the-night wakings is very similar to dealing with sleep refusal. Unfortunately, at 2 in the morning you may lack the stamina to follow through with the plan you so confidently plotted when you were awake and rational at 7 in the evening. All of us have arousals from time to time during the night. Fortunately, most children know how to put themselves back to sleep without help. Unfortunately, yours may not.

Reread Chapters 6 and 7 and consider as many causes of night waking that seem appropriate to your situation. After you have ruled out illness as the cause of your child's wakening, think about fatigue. Remember that if your child has become overtired he will be more likely to wake at night.

> *If your child has become overtired, he is more likely to wake at night.*

Consequently, your next step is to make certain that he is getting enough rest. Has his bedtime crept too late? Has he dropped a nap prematurely? Has his schedule become too hectic? Work on correcting these problems and the night wakings may completely disappear or at least become less frequent.

Even a well-rested child will have night wakings from time to time. What should you do at 2 in the morning? If your child is still in his crib, try as hard as you can to leave him there. For example, if he is standing up, lay him back down and rub his back or belly until he calms down but not until he falls asleep. If you have to pick him up to quiet him, put him back in the crib as soon as he settles down. Don't turn on the light and don't take him out of his bedroom—and certainly don't take him into bed with you. Remember, you don't want to foster associations you will regret the next night. In other words, do as little as possible to stop your child's crying and then leave.

If your child has adopted a pacifier and keeps "losing" it or tossing it out of the crib, go out and buy half a dozen pacifiers and put them in a place where he can easily find them. If he somehow manages to pitch all six of these onto the floor, you can feel justified in adopting a cold-turkey approach.

If he complains of thirst, leave four to six ounces of water in a "spillproof" plastic container in the crib or by his bed. If he complains of hunger, the answer is "No food until breakfast." I will assure you again that he won't starve to death before morning.

If your child has graduated to a bed you will have to deal with his nocturnal wanderings. He will probably choose your bedroom as his first destination and may ask to climb in with you. Although allowing him to join you may be the path of least resistance when it is the middle of the night . . .don't. Muster all of the strength you can and walk him back to his bedroom, if he won't go on his own. Do this as often as necessary until the behavior stops.

You may be so tired that you don't wake when your night wanderer climbs into bed with you. If this is happening, or if you find that you are walking your child back to his room more than two or three times each night, you should consider using a gate or latch as I have suggested in the last section, on sleep refusal.

Many children continue to wake once a night even if their parents have managed the problem correctly. If you are successful in getting your child back down in his crib or bed with just a firm reminder that it is nighttime and he needs to go back to sleep, you should probably be happy with that. It won't take too many weeks or months before the behavior will subside. This is particularly true if you have been able to keep the problem from escalating by refusing to negotiate his requests.

On the other hand, if your child is waking multiple times, or if each episode evolves into a "meltdown," you must use either Ferberization or the cold-turkey approach to break the cycle. This is neither fun nor easy in the middle of the night, when you are tired, facing a full workday in the morning, and/or are concerned about keeping the rest of the family well rested. However, gather all of your resources together and do it. If you are consistent it will take only three or four nights, and the results are worth it. The longer you delay in implementing one of these strategies, the more hours of sleep you and your child will lose.

Don't worry about protecting the rest of the family from the crying. I have listened to many parents, usually mothers, who have jeopardized their own health and happiness by staying up with a child just to keep him quiet so the rest of the family could sleep. Remember, you and your child are part of a family, and sometimes every family member must participate in the solution. In the short term, everyone may become a bit sleep-deprived as you encourage the night waker to learn to put himself back to sleep by allowing him to cry. It may help if you all go to bed a bit earlier and trim back your daytime schedules temporarily to make up for lost sleep until the problem is solved. In the long run, the whole family will benefit by having *all* of its members well rested again.

> *Remember, you and your child are part of a family, and sometimes every family member must participate in the sleep solution.*

The Early Riser

When I ask parents if a child sleeps through the night many of them answer, "Well, sort of." Usually what they mean is that the child wakes in the morning, but well before the rest of the family is ready to get up. Of course, "too early" is a definition each family must arrive at for itself. Because I am usually out of the house by 7 to make rounds in the nursery, I wasn't too troubled if our children woke up for the day at 5:30 or 6. However, if you don't leave for work until 8:30, I can see why you might complain if your child is awake at 6:30.

On one hand, you could manage your early riser just the way you would if he woke at 2 A.M. This might mean walking him back to his room and telling him that it is too early to get up. You could just pretend that you don't hear him when he yells from his crib. In other words, you can use the old cold-turkey approach. He might fuss, but eventually your child will realize that if there isn't anything to eat or anyone to play with he might as well just play quietly or go back to sleep for another hour.

Unfortunately, this situation does not lend itself very well to the traditional Ferberization technique, which can be time-consuming. For example, if your child wakes at 5:30 and you begin by adding five or ten minutes of waiting time before you go into his room to settle him, you will have made only four trips back in before it is time for the whole family to get up. This is usually not enough repetitions to alter his waking behavior.

If you wish to use a gradual approach, it might work better for you to wait only five or ten minutes longer each morning before you allow your child to start his day. For example, on Monday you let him cry from 5:30 until 5:40, on Tuesday you wait until 5:50, and so on until you are waiting until 6:30, which is the time you have decided to define as family wake-up. In a week or two your little early riser will get the message.

If the sun is already up when your child is waking prematurely, you can try to darken the room with more opaque shades and/or blankets or bedspreads taped or hung over the windows.

• • •

There is another approach to the early riser that I suggest you consider. It is the if-you-can't-beat-'em-join-'em philosophy. Instead of frustrating yourself by trying to squeeze an extra hour or hour and a half of sleep out of your child in the morning, maybe the whole family should start the day earlier. Now, let me make it very clear that I am not talking about 4:30 or 5 A.M. Although many of the families of shipbuilders and lobstermen here on the coast of Maine are forced into routines that begin that early, I suspect that early hour won't work for your family if you live in a metropolitan area. However, I am suggesting that by getting up forty-five minutes or an hour earlier you could create an opportunity for what might be referred to as "quality time."

Instead of allowing your two-year-old to stay up past his natural and healthy bedtime of 7 so that he can play with (and unfortunately be overstimulated by) Dad, who arrives home from work at 6:45, why not have a "family bed" half hour from 6 to 6:30 in the morning? I can hear your gasp of incredulity. Is this the same pediatrician who cautioned us on page after page about the ills of co-sleeping? Yes, it is. I am not advocating co-sleeping, I am merely suggesting that it might be fun for you all to get together under the covers for some family time together first thing in the morning. Kids love it. Some of my fondest memories both as a child and as a parent are those fifteen or twenty minutes in the mornings when we talked, tussled, and played games in bed before we started the day.

With an earlier start breakfast could become a more leisurely sit-down family event instead of a rushed grab-an-English-muffin-and-a-cup-of-coffee free-for-all. Children tend to have better appetites early in the day, and I often suggest that parents

> *Do not put your child to bed later at night so that he will sleep longer in the morning! It does not work . . .period. In fact, it will usually make things worse. You may trade early rising for middle-of-the-night waking, or more likely you will get both plus some daytime crankiness to boot. Go back to the chart on page 18. Calculate how much sleep your child is getting and compare it to how much he needs. If you discover that you are expecting him to sleep longer at night than is average for his age, you can try to abolish early waking with a later bedtime, but usually this ploy is not successful.*

of picky eaters make breakfast a more significant meal both nutritionally and socially. This takes time and often means that the whole family must get up earlier.

You may complain that you already find it difficult to get out of bed in the morning because you feel so tired. It may be hard to imagine getting up any earlier to have some quality family time. I suspect that you are currently staying up too late at night. How are you spending your evenings? Are the TV shows you are watching of sufficient value to warrant losing an hour of sleep? Try giving *yourself* a healthy bedtime. Remember, a good parent has to be well rested. Ben Franklin was right; early-to-bed-and-early-to-rise has its advantages. Instead of seeing your child's early rising as a negative, think of it as a wake-up call to reorganize your life so that you can have some quality family time in the morning. Your children are usually at their best in the morning. Take advantage of this fact and start your day an hour earlier so you can enjoy it with them.

Falling Back and Springing Ahead

Twice each year we mess with Mother Nature and turn the clocks forward or back an hour. These changes to and back from Daylight Saving Time may raise havoc with your child's carefully crafted sleep schedule. On the other hand, there may be some situations when tampering with the clock will actually help your child go to bed earlier or sleep longer. Over the long haul it will probably come out a wash.

Most of the time children will adjust to the time change promptly if the rest of the family makes all of the appropriate adjustments in their schedules. In other words, this is one situation where going cold turkey is the first choice. After all, it is only an hour. However, if your child is not adapting well to a shift to or from Daylight Saving, gradually shift his schedule in the direction you want to go by ten minutes a day. He probably won't notice, and in a week you will have regained the lost hour. Remember, by keeping your child's bedroom as dark as possible you will keep him from being fooled by the longer days of late spring and early summer.

When a Family Divides

Even in an amicable divorce fatigue can become a serious issue. With one in three marriages ending in divorce, it is not surprising that many of the children in my practice have parents who don't live together. Unfortunately, fatigue is often associated with this arrangement. The most frequent problem that I have observed occurs when a child is returned to his custodial parent at the end of a visitation significantly sleep-deprived. This fatigue usually manifests itself as cranky, irritable, and irrational behavior. The child may be verbally abusive to the custodial parent or appear sullen and withdrawn. Sometimes this behavior is mistakenly attributed to alleged propaganda from the noncustodial parent. I am not naive. I realize that occasionally, even though they know it is a mistake, divorced parents may badmouth their "ex" in front of the child. However, I am also sure that many times the things said by the child at the end of a visitation are said out of a combination of anger about the divorce and the exhaustion caused by the visitation. The sleep-deprived child often doesn't mean what he says.

> *The sleep-deprived child often doesn't mean what he says.*

Some children are so fatigued by their weekend visitations that it takes them until mid-week to recover. For the school-age child this can have an adverse effect on school performance. Headaches, nocturnal leg pains, and the other physical symptoms of fatigue I have discussed in other chapters can become quite troublesome.

There are several reasons that a child shuttling back and forth between two parents can become fatigued. First, he has two places to sleep, two beds with which to bond. The bed at his primary residence may always be his favorite, and he may always sleep better there. Bedwetting is a good example of how this difference in comfort level can manifest itself. The noncustodial parent may accuse the other parent of poor parenting because the child never wets on visitation but is a notorious bedwetter in his primary residence. The explanation is simple. In his usual bed the child sleeps more deeply—in fact, so deeply that he is not awakened by the urge to void and so wets the bed. When the child is on a visitation he is not completely comfortable in that bed and so will not sleep deeply enough to wet. This same phenomenon can occur when visiting Grandma as well. Eventually, after enough nights at the noncustodial house, he will probably start to wet there, too.

Normal bedtimes are sometimes not maintained when the child is with the noncustodial parent. Often this is simply because of different household schedules (older stepchildren in the house, for an example). More often the noncustodial parent keeps the child busy in an understandable attempt to maximize the limited time they have together. Weekends filled with trips to the zoo, wonderful hours at the playground, and visiting the noncustodial extended family can be exhausting. The fatigue can be compounded when bedtimes are pushed back by an extra video or a trip to the movies.

In some families the roles are reversed. The custodial house may be more hectic and disorganized, and the child's bedtime too late. For this child the trip to the noncustodial parent can be like a bit of R&R, with a quieter lifestyle, a healthier bedtime, and more opportunity to rest.

It can be difficult to balance your natural desire to spend time with your child against his need for sleep, particularly when you don't get to see him every day. However, there are solutions to the sleep deprivation inherent in the situation of a divided family. First, both parents must understand and accept the importance of the child's sleep requirements. This means that the child's sleep and nap schedule must be high on the priority list when visitations are planned. The child needs to have a comfortable, secure, and quiet place to sleep at both his custodial and noncustodial homes. Both parents must resist the temptation to fill every hour with good times. There will be many other visits as the months and years pass. Both parents should attempt to transfer the child to the other parent in a well-rested state or early enough in the day so that the child can still get to bed near his usual time.

> *Both parents must understand and accept the importance of their child's sleep requirements.*

When the terms of the divorce are being negotiated/mediated, realistic schedules should be considered that include time for the child to rest. Although both parents may agree that they want shared custody, with the child splitting up the weekdays between households, work schedules, commuting times, and distances from schools may make this simply impractical from the child's standpoint. If the arrangement means that a six-year-old will be going to bed at 9 P.M. on school nights half of the time, there is a problem. Ideally an arrangement can be worked out that seems fair to both parents and allows the child enough time to sleep and rest. However, it is more important that the child have a healthy bedtime than that he spend an exactly equal amount of time with each parent.

Occasionally even in amicable divorces unrealistic custodial arrangements come out of well-meaning courts and mediators' offices. I usually recommend that parents consult a pediatrician or some other expert in child care to see if the visitation or custodial schedule they are considering leaves enough time for the child to rest and sleep. If there are issues that can't be resolved, the child should have his own legal representation (known as a guardian ad litem). Divorce is never a happy experience, but by keeping your child's sleep needs in mind the transition between households can become a more positive one.

Summary of Strategies

- If your child refuses to go to sleep in his own bed, begin by agreeing to sit on his bed, then in a chair next to his bed. Each night move the chair closer to the door.

- If all else fails, put a latch on your child's bedroom door.

- Night wakings may be a sign that your child is overtired. Consider an earlier bedtime.

- If you can't solve your child's early waking by ignoring his complaints, consider starting your day earlier and going to bed earlier yourself.

- Consider the child's sleep needs when negotiating/mediating a divorce settlement.

- Visitation schedules should leave enough time (including time for travel) for the child to rest and sleep.

- Each house should have an environment conducive to good sleep.

- Parents should resist the temptation to fill every day with activities.

- Each parent should strive to return the child to the other parent in a well-rested state.

9

The More the Wearier

The Challenge of Raising More Than One Well-Rested Child

Although there are some things in life, such as a barn raising, that get easier when more people are involved, keeping your family well rested is unfortunately not one of them. Keeping your child and yourself well rested has been difficult, and your decision to have another child is asking for even more trouble . . .but do it anyway. There are plenty of strategies you can learn to keep your enlarging family from becoming sleep-deprived. Your first challenge is going to come as soon as the new baby gets home from the hospital.

Where Is the New Baby Going to Sleep?

Don't forget what you read in Chapter 5. If your older child is still in a crib, don't displace her until she is crawling out or asks to move to a big girl's bed. Remember, her crib may have become an important security object that can help her weather those first trying months as she learns to accept the inevitability of becoming a sibling.

> *Don't force your child out of her crib so that her younger sibling can use it.*

If you are fortunate enough to have bedrooms for everyone, I hope that you will have the new baby sleeping in her own room before the first week (if not the first night) is over. Reread Chapter 2 if you don't remember why sharing a bedroom with an infant is a bad idea.

If you don't have enough bedrooms to go around you need to explore your options again. First, reexamine your house or apartment. Is there some way you can reassign the space so that everyone can have a room with a door? Be creative. This is an important problem to solve if you are going to continue to have a rested family.

Who Is Going to Share a Room with a New Baby?

This is the next question to answer if you can't figure out how to give everyone a separate space to sleep. There is no one best answer. Your older child may be a good sleeper, either because you helped her learn sleep independence or just because she is a natural. In this case the new baby and her older sibling could share a room. However, big sister must be trustworthy. You don't want to discover that four-year-old Elizabeth has carried three-week-old Martha down to the family room at 3 in the morning so that they can both watch a video.

If the older child can be trusted but is not a terribly sound sleeper, I still suggest that your first option should be to have the siblings share a room. You may be pleasantly surprised at how compatible they can be. The older child will often sleep through the usual commotion that accompanies an infant's nocturnal feedings. Ideally, you will quickly relearn the skills of nursing a baby and changing diapers by the dim glow of a small night-light to keep the disturbance to a minimum.

If your older child is a very light sleeper, you may have to set up the baby's crib in your bedroom. Obviously this is not your first choice, but perhaps you can create a darkened corner using drapes or screens to minimize the visual and auditory interference between your infant and her parents.

Wherever you put her crib, the new baby may have trouble settling in and learning to put herself to sleep even though you have carefully read and reread the first four chapters of this book. I have warned you that there is some luck involved. Eventually your new baby will learn sleep independence, but remember, it may mean allowing her to cry for a while. This may take only three or four nights, but it could be a week or two.

During this "training period" you might find it easier to temporarily shuffle beds and cribs and move your older child into your bedroom. This arrangement will allow you to let the baby cry in a separate room and keep the disruption to everyone else's sleep to a minimum. Just place big sister's mattress on the floor in your room, or if she is still in a crib, set up the crib in a corner. Remember, we don't want this temporary solution to degenerate into co-sleeping.

Resist the temptation to allow the new baby to sleep in the living areas of the house during the daytime. Remember that you want to simplify the settling-in process by providing the infant with only one location for sleeping. Also, keep in mind the old adage "out of sight, out of mind." Your first child may still be struggling with the ambivalence that often comes with being thrust into the role of sibling. If you allow the new baby to sleep in the family room, her presence will be a constant reminder to her older sister that she is no longer numero uno. When you put the baby down in a bedroom, the older child has more opportunities to bask in the glow of your unshared attention. This simple rule can help you keep the inevitable sibling rivalry to a minimum.

Don't allow the new baby to sleep in the living areas during the day.

Maintaining Your Older Child's Bedtime

If you have been successful in creating a pleasant end-of-the-day ritual and a healthy bedtime for your first child, it would be a shame to have all your good work at raising a well-rested child go down the tubes when the new baby comes home. You will find that the older child may be very resistant to going to bed if her younger sibling is still up and about. She won't want to miss anything exciting that might happen after she goes to sleep. She may understand that the baby will wake and feed later at night, but your older child may find it very unsettling to go to bed and leave her younger sibling to enjoy your undivided attention.

This unfortunate fact of family life can present a serious problem. Babies need to be fed frequently, and their erratic schedules may not mesh comfortably with your older child's bedtime in the beginning. Do the best you can. Establish the 7-to-7 lights-out rule (see Chapter 3) for the baby. Try your hardest to have her in her crib, in her room, with the door shut and the lights out, by the time it is the older child's bedtime.

If this arrangement just isn't happening, don't give up. Keep it near the top of your time-management priorities, and you will get there eventually. While you are waiting for the new baby to settle in to an early bedtime, try to create a bedtime ritual that is most acceptable to your first child under the circumstances. Allow her to choose which parent she wants to participate in each part of the ritual, and remember that this may change from night to night without any rhyme or reason. However, don't let the process drag on too long. If you didn't have time for a one-hour ritual before, you certainly don't now that you are the parent of two children. Reread the sections in Chapter 4 about building and maintaining bedtime rituals.

> *Try to have the new baby already in bed well before her older sibling's bedtime.*

If the baby is due for a feeding during your older child's bedtime ritual, try to put her off with a pacifier. If she is bottle-fed, obviously one parent can do this while the other is putting big sister to bed. If the baby is breastfed, this may be a good opportunity to use a bottle of pumped breast milk or even formula. Although I am strong advocate of breastfeeding, I think that maintaining your older child's bedtime might have to take precedence over nursing for that one feeding. Remember, I am talking about a very temporary arrangement of several days or a couple of weeks at most until schedules begin to shake out. Keep your older child's bedtime a top priority. Life for everyone will be much happier if you can.

Even if you are successful in getting big sister down on time, she may pop up from time to time to make sure that she isn't missing a family party to which she hasn't been invited. Be firm in returning her to bed. However, make sure that you create the impression that nothing interesting is happening even though the baby may be up feeding. Don't use these evening hours to play actively with the new baby. Remember, you don't want to overstimulate her at this hour of the day, and you don't want her older sibling to hear the unmistakable noises of a good time being had by all (well, almost all) while she is supposed to be sleeping.

Meshing Daytime Schedules

Once you have gotten the siblings settled into their own sleeping quarters and reestablished the older one's bedtime ritual, your next challenge will be to coordinate their daytime schedules. Unless your first child is still under age two when the new baby is born, she has probably begun to sprout the wings of a social butterfly. She has become accustomed to going to the library on Mondays for story hour and to Rachel's house on Tuesdays for playgroup. Wednesdays she has Gymboree, and Thursdays she has swimming lessons. She may be going to preschool three mornings a week, or she may be in grade school and have soccer practice most afternoons.

The problem is that the new baby needs to be sleeping most of the day. How are you going to get big sister to all of the activities she has come to enjoy and continue to keep the baby well rested? This can be a serious problem, one that is probably unique to our North American society, which can offer such a wide variety of diversions to its children.

I can only suggest some solutions I have seen work for other parents. First, you can hope that your new baby is one of those rare, flexible, and amiable children who quickly learn to accept their cribs but are also willing to sleep in any environment. She may be perfectly happy to doze in the car, on the bleachers at the swimming pool, or in the noisy nursery at the health club. These unusual children are born and not made. If you are lucky enough to have one it will be much easier for you to allow your older child to keep up with her activities. However, be careful not to allow yourself to slip into denial if the baby starts to show signs of sleep deprivation. If she begins to have unexplained fussy spells or her sleep patterns at home become erratic, you must rethink toting her along as you chauffeur her older sibling to activities all over town.

It is much more likely that your new baby will not take kindly to having her natural sleep patterns interrupted by trips out of the house to soccer games and playgroups. Your first step should be backward for a long look at the older sibling's activities. How many of them are really beneficial? Has she become overcommitted? Is she one of the "hurried" children you will read about in Chapter 10? Maybe the arrival of your second child will serve as a wake-up call that it is time to reprioritize your family schedule. Should you eliminate some of the activities that are more tiring than they are enriching?

> **Schedule your older child's activities around her young sibling's naps, not the other way around.**

Of course, there is a wide variety of arrangements you can patch together that will allow your older child to continue to attend her favorite activities while her younger sibling is sleeping. Two of these are hiring someone to come into your home to watch the baby and carpooling with other parents. Some options may be costly and others may be a nuisance to organize. However, I hope that I have convinced you that keeping your children well rested is worth the hassle and expense involved.

These can be difficult decisions. How important is it to keep your infant well rested? Is it okay for your infant to endure a little sleep deprivation so that your toddler can enhance her social skills? I don't have all the answers. I can only hope to alert you to the fact that these are the kinds of questions a skillful parent should be asking herself on a daily basis. Reread Chapters 1, 6, and 7 to help you identify the symptoms of fatigue that might help you decide how to balance your younger child's sleep requirements and your older child's need for social and educational stimulation.

Different Strokes for Different Folks

Within a few days after the birth of your new baby it should become very obvious that you have not cloned your first child. Fortunately, we are all unique individuals and have inherited our own special mix of our parents' DNA. Your first attempts at raising a well-rested child may have gone easily because you were blessed with a baby who didn't need any help in learning sleep independence. She was a natural. On the other hand, your second child may have been born with a less-mellow disposition. While her older sibling may be able to sleep anytime and anywhere, the second addition (or edition) to your family may not tolerate any changes in her routine.

We all respond differently when we become sleep-deprived. One of your children might become tearful and clingy when she gets tired, while the other one may have violent tantrums. Some children will just curl up in a corner when they are fatigued and others will become hyperactive. Each of your children will have her own sleep requirement and tolerance for fatigue. The sooner you learn and accept these differences, the easier your job of raising two or three well-rested children will be.

> *Each of your children will have her own sleep requirement and tolerance for fatigue.*

It may be more difficult to get your children to accept these differences. For example, if your ten-year-old has always needed more sleep than her seven-year-old sister, she may find it very difficult to admit that she should go to bed half an hour earlier. It can be one of those macho-sibling-rivalry sort of struggles.

You could try to slyly move the younger sister's bedtime earlier and extend her bedtime ritual by letting her read for an hour, but she may not fall for this ploy. If the older child exhibits symptoms such as severe headaches that *you* can clearly attribute to fatigue, your job is to convince *her* that the association exists. Help her understand that she isn't a wimp because she needs more sleep than her younger sibling. If she balks, tell her that she can stay up later but that she had better not complain when she has one of her headaches. Ideally, she will learn sooner rather than later that her sleep is more important than having a later bedtime than her younger sister.

Unfortunately, many children reach adulthood seemingly without a clue about their own sleep needs and their tolerance for fatigue. Part of raising a well-rested child is helping her understand her own uniqueness in general, but particularly when it comes to sleep.

Summary of Strategies

- Don't force your child out of her crib so that a new sibling can use it.

- Work hard to provide each child with her own sleeping space.

- Put the new baby in a bedroom to sleep during the daytime.

- Put the new baby to bed before her older sibling's bedtime.

- Try to schedule your older child's activities around her young sibling's naps, not the other way around.

10

FATIGUE AND YOUR SCHOOL-AGED CHILD

Sleeping Boy Left Aboard School Bus

Five-year-old Dewey Ogg was left on the bus last Wednesday when the driver finished her trip and failed to notice him asleep on a seat. Temperatures were in single digits when the bus was parked in a lot off Windham Center Road.

Portland (Maine) *Press Herald*, January 25, 1994

Fortunately, Dewey was discovered alive and well four and a half hours later. As you can imagine, there was a considerable amount of finger-pointing and a request for a thorough review of school policies in the wake of this incident. However, young Master Ogg's school bus snooze was not an isolated event. Since reading this article in our local paper, I have become aware of three other nearly identical incidents that have occurred over the last five years. Two were also here in Maine, and the other took place in Massachusetts. In each case the child was a kindergartner who fell asleep on the bus ride to or from school. I suspect that this scenario has been repeated multiple times in other parts of the country.

As I read through the newspaper reports of each incident, I was impressed that while each bus driver's oversight was discussed in detail, there was no mention of why the children had fallen asleep on the bus. What were their bedtimes? Did they have to be awakened in the morning so that they could be dropped off at day care by their parents on the way to work? As you read in Chapter 1, if your child falls asleep in the car it means that he is sleep deprived. Clearly, these three children had been sent off to school underslept. A well-rested child would not have fallen asleep on the bus.

Unfortunately, Dewey Ogg and his fellow school bus snoozers are just the tip of an iceberg of fatigued children who are showing up in school each day poorly prepared to learn. Some of them doze off in class. Some appear distractible. Others fall asleep on the bus—but unlike Dewey wake up in time to get off at their stops. Thousands of other children just don't learn up to their potential because they are too tired.

You have helped your child learn to put himself to sleep in his own bed. You may have avoided colic and gotten through the not-so-terrible twos relatively unscathed because of your careful attention to nap preservation. But don't let down your guard. As your child enters school you and he will face new assaults to his stamina. If you want him to be a successful and well-mannered student, he must continue to be well rested. This chapter will alert you to some of the new symptoms of sleep deprivation that you may not have experienced with your preschooler, and I will warn you about some special situations that can make your school-age child fatigued. The solutions remain similar to those you employed when he was younger, but as you might expect, there will be some new wrinkles.

> *If you want your child to be a successful and well-mannered student, he must continue to be well-rested.*

School Can Be Exhausting

Although we often read and hear complaints that public schools are not as academically demanding today as they were a generation or two ago, you must not forget that a day, or even a half day, in school can really wear down your child. If he is highly motivated he may feel that attending school is like being onstage from the moment he walks into class until the last bell of the day has rung. Everyone is watching him, and the teacher and his fellow students are expecting him to perform. He must be prepared to raise his hand if he knows the answer to a question. If he wants to do well, every minute counts and he must present his best side. At home he can sit down and mellow out for a few minutes to catch his breath and recharge his emotional and physical batteries. Not so in school. If he begins to daydream or relax for just a minute he may miss out on something important—or even worse, be reprimanded for not paying attention. A day in school for the highly motivated child can drain his energy tank dry. Even though he may not have been active physically he will be tired by mid-afternoon, if not before. All of that thinking and concentrating can be mentally exhausting.

On the other hand, if your child is a social butterfly and not terribly interested in what the teacher has planned for him, school can also be exhausting. A class of twenty-five other children and a playground full of ten or twenty times more potential playmates provide a fertile environment for overstimulation. If his teacher allows the class to be relatively unstructured, his activity level may be allowed to grow unchecked. On the other hand, if the teacher tries to rein in the free spirits in her class with an excess of rules and consequences, your less-motivated child must continue to battle his natural urges to explore and interact with his peers.

In either case your child will probably finish the school day drained of energy. A long bus ride home with fifty other fidgety and noisy children may be the straw that breaks the camel's back. He may arrive home and surprise you by asking to take a nap. On the other hand, his fatigue may cause him to act unusually cranky or active.

It is not unusual for children to begin wetting the bed again when school starts in the fall. Although I have heard some so-called experts on child behavior ascribe this to some ill-defined "stress," I think it is almost always the result of fatigue. The school day has been so exhausting that the child sleeps through the urge to get up and void. Once the child becomes more rested and more acclimated to the school schedule, the bedwetting usually resolves.

You may have been reasonably successful in keeping your preschooler well rested. Although you may have allowed him to stay up for a few hours after dinner so that you could play with him, he was able to sleep longer in the morning or enjoy a siesta or even a late-afternoon R&R to recoup his losses. However, with your child's entry into school you and he must adhere to a new schedule. The school board makes the schedule, and it probably won't allow you the luxury of a later bedtime. School is tiring, and it gobbles up time that you may not have budgeted. It is time to relook at your schedules and do some reprioritization.

The Challenge of Afternoon Kindergarten

In many parts of this country kindergarten is a half-day event. Based on the correct assumption that some five-year-olds don't have the stamina for a six- or seven-hour school day, children attend either a morning or an afternoon session. Unfortunately, these arrangements have several drawbacks. In an attempt to get two classes into one day, the actual classroom time may be so shortened by bus rides and the time-consuming task of dressing and undressing the little neophytes that the educational experience may be suboptimal.

> *Many kindergarten-age children should still be napping in the afternoon.*

The more troubling consequence of the half-day kindergarten arrangement is that half of the children may be forced to go to school after lunch, which is a portion of the day when they are likely to be very tired. Biologically, most of us are programmed to be sleepy after our midday meal. Many five-year-olds, and a few six-year-olds, will still nap after lunch if they are given the opportunity, even if they seem to be getting enough sleep at night.

Obviously, this midday drowsiness is more likely to occur if your child is going to bed too late or being forced to wake too early in the morning.

If you have followed the suggestions in Chapter 5, you have taken advantage of this natural dip in your child's biorhythms and helped him preserve his after-lunch nap/siesta as long as possible. However, if your child has had the misfortune of being assigned to afternoon kindergarten your efforts at keeping him well rested may be severely challenged. Your child might be one of the lucky ones who has developed enough stamina by his fifth birthday that he is able to handle afternoon kindergarten without any obvious difficulties. On the other hand, your child may arrive in class after lunch each day biologically more prepared to take a snooze than to learn and behave. The problem may go unnoticed until he falls asleep on the school bus and misses his stop—just like Dewey Ogg on that cold school bus. Or your child may have trouble learning his letters and numbers because he is too tired to concentrate. The teacher may complain that he is not following directions or that he is getting into altercations with his classmates. She may not realize that part of the problem is his natural after-lunch sleepiness.

What can you do? What are your options when an afternoon kindergarten assignment threatens to sabotage your attempts at raising a well-rested child? The first thing you can try is a direct appeal to the principal or district administrator. You can explain how important you feel it is for your child to arrive at school alert and ready to learn. Enlist your pediatrician's help. Ask her to write a supportive letter. March into the principal's office with this little book in hand and politely wave it in his or her face. When you are on a mission it never hurts to have a visual aid.

Obviously, some parents discovered how important rest is for their children long before I ever wrote this book, and I am sure that some school districts are inundated with requests for morning kindergarten. In an attempt to be equitable many districts flip-flop the classes at mid-year and refuse to hear any requests for special arrangements. You might even organize other parents and advocate to abolish afternoon kindergarten and replace it with a slightly longer morning class. Unfortunately, creating this arrangement often becomes a money issue, no question about it. I hope this book's influence will grow to the point that more parents, voters, taxpayers, and school administrators will realize how important it is that classes be filled with well-rested children.

If you fail in all of your attempts to have your child placed in morning kindergarten, you will be forced to rely on a patchwork of strategies to keep him well rested enough to function optimally in the afternoon. You could let him sleep as late as possible in the morning. This may be difficult to blend with the schedules of other family members, not to mention the natural inclination of young children to wake early. Or you could feed your child a very early lunch and then impose an after-lunch siesta that would begin early enough so that he will be rejuvenated in time to head off to school well rested.

Regardless of whether you chose to adjust wake-ups or reintroduce a siesta, it is extremely important to do everything else that you can to keep your child well rested in the hope of minimizing his after-lunch sleepiness. This includes adhering to healthy bedtimes, which means a consistent and succinct ritual. Pay careful attention to schedules and avoid overfilling them with activities that will siphon off energy your child will need to do well in school. Read your child's behavior carefully. Use what you have learned about identifying symptoms of fatigue and then take prompt action to get him more sleep. Afternoon kindergarten can be a disaster for some children, but if you stay on your toes you can help your child make the best of a bad situation.

Grumpy Young Men (and Women)

I once assumed that it was common knowledge that fatigue is the most frequent cause of cranky behavior. At least that is what my mother taught me. However, I continue to encounter parents who are worried that their grumpy child has some undiscovered medical illness or a serious psychological disturbance. Most of the time the child is underslept and when given the chance to get more rest will begin to behave in a more acceptable manner.

> *Fatigue is the most frequent cause of cranky behavior.*

There are other causes of cranky behavior in school-age children, including marital discord, academic failure due to learning disabilities, mental illness, and even drug dependency. However, if your school-age child is more grouchy than you would like, particularly if his behavior degenerates as the day wears on, your first response should be to reevaluate his sleep habits. An earlier bedtime and a quieter day are likely to help and are certainly inexpensive first steps.

Like adults, children come in three flavors. Some of them seem happy and upbeat regardless of how dismal their surroundings. Others appear to be very easily angered and frustrated, while the majority of children have a disposition that seems to ebb and flow with the atmosphere that surrounds them. All of us will eventually react to fatigue with negative behavior. Some of us just seem to arrive in this world with shorter fuses and will explode more violently when exhausted. You and I aren't going to change the unique mix of genetic material that your child has inherited. If he is mellow and rarely gets grouchy even when he is getting tired, just thank your lucky stars. However, if your child is prone to spells of grumpiness, accept that as the cards he (and you) have been dealt. You won't be able to change his spots, but you can help him put his best face forward more of the time by keeping him well rested.

We all have two personalities: the one that other people like and a darker side that appears when we are overtired. Some children can hold their crankiness in check when they are in school or some other public place even though they are nearing exhaustion. But watch out! Once they enter the more tolerant and familiar surroundings of home, all hell breaks loose; they relax their grip on their dark side, and it runs wild.

The result may be merely unpleasant crankiness and whining or full-fledged tantrums may erupt. Although you have already read about tantrums in Chapter 5, they deserve some additional attention in this chapter about school-aged children because they might be so severe that you wonder if your child has a serious psychological problem. He might say and do things that are completely out of character, and at times he may seem totally irrational. While behavior like this can be symptomatic of a psychiatric disturbance, it is more likely the result of fatigue. First, assess your child's sleep needs and see if things improve when your child is more rested. However, you should discuss the situation with your pediatrician. She may suggest an electroencephalogram (also known as an EEG or brain wave test), because tantrumlike behavior may rarely be a symptom of a seizure disorder. She may also recommend that you and your child visit a psychologist or psychiatrist. In recent years some physicians have successfully managed children who are prone to rage outbursts with a variety of medications. You can begin to work at improving your child's sleep schedule while the medication is being tried, or you may want to give fatigue prevention a try for a few months before you consider a pharmacologic solution.

You have probably already discovered that during a tantrum attempts at discussion or education are a waste of time. Your best approach is to get your child into his room, by force if necessary, until things have quieted down. You may want to physically restrain him until it passes. One pediatrician in South Carolina calls this technique the "Big Hug." It should be done in a caring manner in an attempt to protect your child and the environment and comfort him until it passes. It is very likely that he may fall asleep at the end of the tantrum. After your child has recovered and is rested, maybe even the next day, you may return to the issue that triggered the outburst. Often the straw that broke the camel's back is so trivial than no one can even recall it. There is no sense in trying to get to the root of the problem until the child is over his fatigue and more receptive. Tantrums can stir up strong emotions, and everyone concerned needs to cool down, get a good night's sleep, and give the situation a fresh look when the sun comes up in the morning.

Poor School Performance

Many children who are doing poorly in school have some degree of learning disability. However, there are some children who are not working up to their capabilities as the result of a disturbed family environment, such as a pending divorce. Tragically, some children do poorly in school because their parents are not supportive of the educational system. Fortunately, most parents give their children's education a high priority. Regardless of the strength of his learning capabilities or the amount of support he derives from his family, your child will not learn up to his potential if he goes to school sleep-deprived.

> *Regardless of the strength of his learning capabilities, your child will not learn up to his potential if he goes to school sleep-deprived.*

While this seems like a rather obvious statement of fact, I have been unable to find much scientific research to support it until just the last few years. I guess this is just another example of sleep's getting "no respect." There are plenty of studies documenting the relationship between nutrition and learning. I guess the association between being well rested and school performance was just too intuitive to attract scientific attention. However, in September 1998 a study was published that investigated nearly three hundred first-graders who were doing poorly in school. More than fifty of the children were determined to have disordered sleep because of upper airway obstruction (see Chapter 7, page 131). Half of these children underwent surgery to remove their tonsils and adenoids. Their sleep patterns and their school performance both improved. Although there could be many explanations for this, it certainly seems to support an observation that schoolteachers have made for generations. The student who isn't getting enough sleep will probably do poorly.

Sometimes the problem is obvious because the child nods off in class. In the case of an older child it is tempting to pass off this behavior as a response to a boring teacher, but when a first-grader puts his head down on his desk and falls asleep, it is hard to mistake the problem. Having gone to school for twenty-two of my first thirty years, I certainly understand that teachers can be boring. However, don't be too quick to defend your child's disinterest in his classwork as boredom, even if you "know" that he is very bright. Some of the problem may be motivation, but give a thought to his sleep schedule. If he has more trouble in his afternoon classes, fatigue may be the problem. A boring class is just like a ride in the car. If your child is well rested he should be able to stay awake even if the teacher is a drone.

Tubed Out and Tired Out

Like most pediatricians I find that children in this country spend far too much of their time watching television. It is the passive and sedentary nature of TV and not the content of the shows that is the problem. If a child spends three or four (or often many more) hours each day watching other people do things, this doesn't speak well for the quality of his existence. In today's vernacular, he needs to "get a life." The child in front of the TV is watching someone else's life and not his own. Video games are only slightly better in that they at least require some participation, but they are still basically sedentary in nature.

What does this have to do with sleep? To sleep well at night it helps to have been both physically and mentally active during the day. Physicians often suggest to older adults who are having trouble sleeping that they get more exercise during the day so that they will be more appropriately tired when night falls. The activity seems to be even more beneficial if it takes place outdoors—in addition to warding off depression, there may be something about sunlight striking our faces that helps keep our internal clocks running smoothly. In other words, if you would like your child to be healthy he must have an appropriate mix of physical activity, good diet, and sleep. Allowing your child to "tube out" for hours at a time is not setting up this good balance.

> *For a child to be healthy he must have an appropriate mix of physical activity, good diet, and sleep.*

One recent study has revealed that children who watch more television during the day and/or at bedtime were more likely to have problems sleeping. These problems included refusing to go to bed, difficulty falling asleep, anxiety about sleep, and a tendency to sleep for shorter periods of time.

These researchers also observed that children who had televisions in their bedrooms were more likely to have sleep problems. One explanation for this is that television viewing can delay a child's bedtime well beyond its natural limits. This situation is very likely to occur when a child is allowed to have a TV in his bedroom and stay up until who-knows-how-late watching it. If your child has a television in his room it is very difficult for you to monitor what he is watching, how long he is watching it, and when he is going to sleep.

Even if you have reasonable control over your child's TV watching habits the networks and advertisers are not going to make it easy for you. Many of the shows that could be loosely described as family entertainment are aired at times well after your child's healthy bedtime. Holiday specials are an unfortunate example of this phenomenon. Of course, this is a big country with four time zones, and to get a maximum audience for the country, shows are often aired at a reasonable time for people in the Midwest. But for those of us on the East Coast, our children will have to stay up an hour or more past their bedtime.

Many teachers will observe that many of their students get really "wired" during holiday seasons. They often attribute this phenomenon to all of the candy that is available. Contrary to popular opinion, there is really no solid proof that sugar causes hyperactivity. A more likely explanation for the phenomenon is that during holiday seasons children are either up late trick-or-treating, going to parties, or watching TV specials well past a healthy bedtime. Some of them arrive in school the next day wound up tighter than a drum as a result of the fatigue.

High-Tech and Low-Tech Solutions to the Tube Problem

First, *don't put a TV in your child's bedroom*—or if he already has one, remove it. This is not cruel or unusual punishment. It is the healthy thing to do. The improvement in your child's sleeping habits will be dramatic.

> *Don't put a TV in your child's bedroom.*

If your child complains that he will miss his favorite shows if he goes to bed at a healthy hour, there is an electronic solution: the VCR. I realize that the thought of having to program your VCR to actually record something may be frightening to you, but don't panic—you can do it. With a little practice and persistence you will be able to tape that holiday special and show it to your child the next evening well before his bedtime. Instead of being a slave to technology, learn to use it to solve problems. Don't stop with the holiday specials. Program your VCR to tape regular TV shows so that you can manipulate time in your favor and for your child's benefit. If the reruns of *Star Trek* come on at 7 and his bedtime is 7:30, just tape them and show them at 6 or 6:30. If you like to sit down and watch the news after dinner, but if you do that pushes your child's bedtime ritual later by half an hour, simply tape the news and view it after he's gone to bed.

If you really want to help your child develop a sensible attitude toward television, I would suggest thinking in terms of the phrase "one is enough." For the school-age child one hour of TV per day is all that child really "needs." Obviously, the child doesn't really "need" any TV, but most of us would find a goal of zero television unrealistic and too difficult to achieve. Total restriction of TV runs the risk of making it into a forbidden fruit and enhancing its inherent magnetism. If it is a rainy weekend day, a reasonable parent can bend the rule a little bit and add half an hour. If your child has misbehaved or is not getting his homework done, the one hour can be removed in increments of half hours. Or if the child has conquered a particularly difficult task or behavior, an extra hour of TV can be added as a reward. When the child is aware that his TV will be limited to an hour each day, he will be quite selective in his choice of shows, usually less junk and more good stuff. You can see that by gaining control over television by using the technology of the VCR and a one-is-enough philosophy, your child is likely to get more sleep, be less sedentary, and make better choices about his viewing diet.

What About Books and Computers?

Too Much of a Good Thing

It might be easy for you to decide what to do when your child is staying up too late watching TV, but what if your child is up past his bedtime reading a book or using a computer for educational purposes? It is difficult to reprimand your child when he is engaged in a mind-expanding activity even though he is losing sleep in the process. I don't have a great answer, but I think you should enter into a dialogue with the child. Tell him you are happy with the way he is spending his evenings but you are concerned because you are seeing evidence of sleep deprivation in his behavior or even school performance. Explore with him how he might budget his time better so that his reading and/or computer work can find a better place in his schedule. If this fails, you may have to set limits on a behavior you would like to encourage, because you know that your child's sleep needs are more important. Teach him that one can overdo a good thing. Your success in helping him moderate his behavior may result in a lesson about priorities that will stay with him for life.

So Much to Do and So Little Time

The Struggle to Protect Your Child from Overinvolvement

Although the failure to maintain a healthy bedtime is the number one cause of fatigue, for many school-aged children an over-filled schedule runs a close second. Even if you succeed in getting your child into bed at what seems like a decent hour, he may still be exhausted because the pace of his days is too hectic. The children of North American suburbia are offered a wider array of organized diversions than any other children on the face of the earth. Sports, both in school and after school; music lessons; dance lessons; Scouts; church groups—the list goes on and on. The temptation to participate in as many activities as possible seems irresistible.

> *An overfilled schedule is a major cause of fatigue for school-aged children.*

Your child wants to try his hand at a variety of sports and do the things his friends are doing. You probably want him to be exposed to as many athletic and cultural experiences as possible. Your parents may not have been able to offer you the chance to take music lessons and play several different sports, and you want to make sure that your child doesn't feel that he is missing out on anything. Like many of us, you may harbor the unrealistic dream that your child will become a college or professional athlete. If that means joining several teams, going to skill camps in the summer, and participating in out-of-season leagues, then that's what will have to be done.

If you haven't already joined the ranks of the minivan-driving parents who spend many afternoons and most of the weekend hustling from one game or practice to the next, you will. Just getting from one activity to another takes time. In some communities practices and games may be scheduled on weekday evenings so that working parents can help with the coaching. Of course, this arrangement compounds the problem by forcing children who may already be overtired to accept a bedtime that is too late.

If your child is like the majority of children in this country, he is going to enjoy much less free time than you did at his age. In a study released in 1998, the Institute for Social Research at the University of Michigan documented just how dramatic this loss has been. For example, in 1981 the children in the survey listed

40 percent of their week as unstructured. However, in 1997 this free time had fallen to 25 percent. Over this same period of time, participation in organized sports nearly doubled, and the time spent running errands or doing housework with parents more than doubled. This increase in time spent with parents certainly doesn't sound like "quality time" and probably results from the fact that more parents are working out of the home and must borrow some of their children's free time to take them shopping. Unfortunately, the loan is seldom repaid.

These changes in the lifestyle of North American children have not gone unnoticed by educators, pediatricians, and child psychologists. Some have used the term "hurried" to describe the child whose life has become filled with activities that adults have organized for him. Afternoons become a race from one structured event to another. Lost in the hustle are opportunities to play independently or organize their own games with playmates.

The tragedy of the hurried and overcommitted child is twofold. The first problem is that with the loss of free time, children lose the opportunity to play, and play has some real educational value. Through play, children can experiment with their own solutions to problems as diverse as how to build an arch out of blocks or how to divide a group of playmates into teams. Play can generate a sense of self-reliance. There are lessons to be learned by participating on a soccer team. However, if that team is part of a league that has been organized by adults, can that activity really be categorized as "play"? Obviously, there should be room in your child's life for both structured "play" and free play, but unfortunately the trend in this country will leave your child little time for self-directed activity.

The second tragedy is that with overcommitment comes the threat of fatigue. Even after your child has outgrown his naps, I am sure, there are several times during the day that, if given the time, he will sit down for what my mom would call a "breather." It may last for a minute and a half, or it may last for half an hour, but it is a period of time during which he can rest and recharge his physical and emotional batteries. He may daydream, or switch to a quiet game. He may even "sleep." Sleep researchers don't define sleep by whether or not our eyes are closed but rather by the pattern of our brain waves. Many of us actually sleep with our eyes open during the day, when those around us think we are just "lost in thought."

If you have allowed your child to become hurried and over-committed, he will have little or no time for these mini-R&R sessions as he is being hustled from activity to activity. He may nod off briefly in the car as he is being rushed from soccer practice to piano lessons and then to a Scout meeting, but this is usually insufficient to refresh him because his day has been so hectic.

Obviously, a hurried or overcommitted child is unlikely to be well rested. You would like your child to enjoy the benefits of organized sports and learn some form of artistic expression. On the other hand, you now understand how important it is for him to be well rested and have ample time for self-directed play. Is there a solution to this dilemma? Well . . . maybe. In some ways it may be like asking for a twenty-six-hour day.

You have already taken a big step toward an answer that may work. The simple act of picking up this book because you were intrigued by its title indicates that you understand a problem exists. Unfortunately, there are hundreds of thousands of parents who don't realize that their children are suffering from fatigue and that the schedule they have structured for them is contributing to the problem. You, on the other hand, have read ten chapters of *Is My Child Overtired?* and you should therefore be sensitive to the issue of sleep deprivation. I hope that without reading another sentence you already have some sense of how you might help your child make decisions about his schedule that will allow him to remain well rested, but let me give you some suggestions.

First, let's be honest. It is going to be difficult. You are swimming against a current of peer pressure and community norms. It is difficult to tell your child that he can't play soccer *and* do Cub Scouts when almost every boy in his class is doing both. You had better have a good reason—and "You will get too tired" probably won't fly very easily.

You can begin by sitting down with your child and having a frank discussion about his schedule. Explore his expectations for each activity. Explain to him why you are worried that he may become overtired if he tries to participate in all the activities he hopes to join. Help him make a priorities list. If you can, remind him of specific examples of what happens to him when he becomes sleep-deprived: headaches, leg pains, grouchy behavior, tantrums.

If you are convinced that his proposed schedule is unworkable, you must lay down the law. Tell him that he must choose from list of reasonable options, and stick to your guns. It should be a lesson well learned and probably learned long before most of his peers have been forced to prioritize their schedules. He may thank you for your foresight when he becomes an adult.

On the other hand, if you think his schedule of activities could be "do-able" if he adheres to a healthy bedtime and is more efficient with the rest of his day, you may wish to negotiate a plan with consequences. For example, tell him that he can join a basketball team and do indoor soccer if his grades stay up and he keeps his grouchy days to two per month. You define what *grouchy* means and give him adequate warning when he is approaching his limit. Another example might be that you allow your child to join the band and the glee club, and do Scouts, but that if you have to wake him with more than a minimal effort more than one day each week he will have to cut one of the activities.

You can ask other parents if they are also concerned about their children's overcommitment and exhaustion. You may be surprised at how many parents share your views and are eager to join you in speaking to the organizers of some of the activities that conflict with a healthy sleep schedule. Together you may be able to hammer out some compromises that will allow your children to participate in several activities each week and not run the risk of becoming exhausted.

These are just a few examples of how you can try to strike a healthy balance between involvement and sleep. I am not going to offer you a quota of how many hours of extracurricular activities you should set as a maximum. The important point is that you must remain vigilant in your effort to make sure that your school-aged child remains well rested and has adequate unstructured time. This means watching for the signs of fatigue that you have read about in Chapters 1 and 6. Then look for solutions: earlier dinners and bedtimes, quiet times after school, shortened commutes. If you have tried these adjustments and your child is still obviously overtired, you must sit down with him and talk about trimming his activities. It won't be fun, but you may be surprised to learn that he has already begun to realize that his day is overfilled and is relieved that you have suggested he cut back. If you have been careful to keep your child's schedule reasonable from the very beginning, the whole process will occur more naturally.

Slumber Parties and Sleepovers

Two of the most popular social activities for many school-aged children are sleepovers and slumber parties. The chance to spend the night at a friend's house and stay up past his usual bedtime is an opportunity to be just a little naughty that your child probably can't resist. There are late-night TV shows to watch, popcorn and pizza to eat, stories to tell, and flashlight games to play. These are nights filled with memories . . . but not much sleep. Like most adults, children often have trouble sleeping in strange places. Of course, it doesn't help matters if your friends are more interested in chatting than sleeping. "Going to bed just a little late" is often not an accurate description of how little sleep your child is going to get at a slumber party. If you allow your child to spend the night at a friend's house you must accept the fact that he will return home the next day sleep-deprived. He may be just a little overtired, or he may be near exhaustion. He may be a little more grouchy than usual, or he may be taken off his feet by a severe headache.

Sleepovers and slumber parties can cause serious sleep deprivation.

Obviously, if your child suffers with severe symptoms of sleep deprivation after he spends the night at a slumber party, you must seriously reconsider whether you will allow him to attend another one. On the other hand, if your child returns home only moderately fatigued, you should plan for some catch-up sleep after the next sleepover. For example, if your child has spent Friday night at a slumber party with three friends, going on an all-day shopping trip to the mall on Saturday is looking for trouble. Plan a quiet day after the sleepover and make it clear that Saturday night won't be a late one.

You may discover that for various reasons your child gets more sleep at some homes than he does at others. Often, this depends on how closely the parents have been monitoring the children, and how successful they have been in enforcing a reasonable bedtime. You may have to be very frank with your child and tell him that he can't sleep over at Zachary's house because he comes home exhausted every time. You can offer to host the sleepover and see if this improves the situation.

Nights spent with friends should be fun and can intensify those friendships. However, they will predictably result in sleep deprivation. By being selective about which homes he may stay at and by allowing ample opportunity for catch-up sleep, you can offer your well-rested child the chance to enjoy these special events.

When your child climbs onto the school bus for the first time he will be taking another step toward independence, but you must still protect him from fatigue. When he arrives at school he will find a new set of challenges that will require energy and concentration to master. Remain vigilant in your efforts to keep him well rested. This will mean preserving a healthy bedtime and protecting him from overinvolvement in extracurricular activities. You will be rewarded by watching your child enjoy and succeed in school.

Summary of Strategies

- If you have the option, choose morning kindergarten.

- If your child must do afternoon kindergarten, allow him to sleep later in the morning or put him to bed earlier. Even better, do both.

- If your child is cranky, assume he is overtired.

- Limit your child to one hour of TV per day and do *not* put a television in his bedroom.

- Use your VCR to record favorite shows and show them at a healthier hour.

- Help your child avoid overcommitment by limiting his participation to a few well-spaced activities.

- Discourage sleepovers and slumber parties, particularly if your child is more vulnerable to sleep deprivation than his peers.

11

TIRED TEENAGERS

Bad News and Good News

As you begin this chapter prepare yourself for some very bad news. No matter how hard you and I try we won't be able to transform your well-rested child into a well-rested teenager. There are just too many forces working against us. Almost by definition adolescents are sleep-deprived. In fact, two sleep researchers (Carskadon and Dement, 1987) have observed that "the truly alert adolescent may be exceptional."

> *Teenagers require at least as much sleep as they did as preadolescents—and probably more.*

On the other hand, the good news is that in at least one part of this country high school administrators have discovered what I have been preaching to you about fatigue. Later in this chapter you will read about how they have made school policy and schedule changes that allow their students to get more sleep and to improve their academic performance. So, while on one hand adolescence may be the black hole of sleep deprivation, there is hope that you may finally be getting some help in your struggle to save your child from exhaustion.

Biology's Bad Joke

Even before you picked up this book you knew that adults need less sleep than children. Like most of us, you probably assumed that this decline in sleep requirement was gradual and steady from birth to age twenty-one. Unfortunately, your assumption is wrong, very wrong. One of the best-kept secrets of human development is that as teenagers progress through adolescence they need increasing amounts of sleep. In fact, researchers have determined that to maintain daytime alertness teenagers need more than nine hours of sleep, compared to the eight hours required by most adults. Sadly, most adolescents are getting less than seven hours of sleep each night.

There is a great temptation to blame inherent laziness for the lack of motivation exhibited by many teenagers, and, in fact, some teenagers *are* lazy. However, there is ample evidence that adolescents require at least as much sleep as they did when they entered puberty, and probably more. To make matters worse, it also appears that many teenagers are naturally inclined to go to bed later and wake up later if they are allowed to set their own schedules. In fact, as they move through adolescence they tend to go to bed later with each passing year. I know that this biologic fact is hard to swallow for those of us who believe that the Eleventh Commandment is Ben Franklin's observations about being "early to bed and early to rise." However, if you are going to cope successfully with your teenager, you must understand that her body's biorhythms have undergone a change for the worse. Don't try to fight it, because it will be just one more poorly chosen battle that you are destined to lose.

Peer and Societal Forces Make Matters Worse

Biology must share some of the blame for tired teenagers with a potpourri of societal forces and peer pressures. Parents naturally relax their control over bedtime schedules as their children enter high school as part of a trend away from micromanagement. In other words, biologic changes encourage your teenager to stay up later, but your parenting style may be allowing it to happen.

Your adolescent can find dozens of exciting things to do late at night, and she has more than enough peers to do them with. Television, the Internet, sports, extracurricular activities, movies, dating, parties, and talking on the phone are just a few. Many teenagers begin to drink large amounts of caffeine-containing drinks that may make it difficult to get sleep even if they aren't up socializing. Sadly, a large percentage begin to drink alcohol, which can also have a negative effect on their sleep patterns.

It has been estimated that between one-half and two-thirds of the high school students in this country work after or before school. Many of these jobs interfere with natural sleep patterns either as a result of their timing or because the teenagers need to stay up later to get their homework completed.

Going from Bad to Worse on the Weekends

Just as the rich get richer and the poor get poorer, teenagers who incur a significant sleep debt during the week often fall further behind because of their weekend sleep habits. By staying up later on Friday and Saturday nights and then sleeping later on Saturday and Sunday mornings, they become vulnerable to what sleep specialists call "sleep phase delay." This condition is similar to jet lag. In fact, some authors have referred to it as "school sleep lag."

> *Teenagers who incur a significant sleep debt during the week often fall further behind because of their weekend sleep habits.*

By going to bed later and sleeping later on the weekend, a teenager reinforces her preferred sleep pattern. However, when Monday comes around her body still expects to be on "weekend time." The greater the discrepancy between her week and weekend schedules the more serious the problem becomes. For the teenager with "school sleep lag," life is similar to that of a long-distance commuter who works in Chicago during the week and spends her weekends enjoying the party scene in Los Angeles. It doesn't take a scientist to tell us that the first few days of the work/school week are going to be a difficult adjustment. Teenagers with school sleep lag are sleepy students and have poorer grades than students who maintain good weekend sleep habits that are more similar to their weekday patterns.

Although we might hope that being forced to wake early for school five days out of seven would quickly minimize the effect of a sleep phase delay, it doesn't happen. A teenager's biologic clock seems to be very stubborn and quite resistant to resetting. In the next section you will learn that sleep lag is just one of the problems intertwined with school schedules.

Out-of-Sync School Starts

In an attempt to keep their transportation costs down most school systems stagger school starting times. The traditional arrangement has the high school and middle school students arriving at school earliest so that the buses can make a second run to pick up and deliver the grade school children. This scheme also allows for ample after-school time for extracurricular activities to meet and athletic teams to practice, but it may require start times as early as 7:15 or 7:30 A.M.

However, there is a very dark side to these early start times. As you have learned, there are numerous biologic and societal factors that force adolescents to go to bed later and need more sleep. It is not surprising that when they are asked to adjust their sleep schedules to conform to a school start that is one or two hours earlier than their natural waking time, teenagers will show up in class sleep-deprived. One researcher found that 20 percent of students fell asleep in class. In another survey, students reported that they were least alert around 10:00 A.M., and 50 percent said that they were most alert at 3:00 P.M., which, of course, is after school has ended for the day.

Therefore, early school start times must be included on the list of contributors to adolescent sleep deprivation. You might argue that if your teenager would just go to bed earlier her sleep patterns would eventually get into sync. Unfortunately, this simply doesn't happen. Scientists have found that students either don't move their bedtimes earlier or if they do the benefit is insignificant. The biologic and societal forces are just too strong.

A Good Idea from the Land of Ten Thousand Lakes

If forcing adolescents to show up at school more than an hour before their natural waking time is filling high school classrooms with grumpy, sleep-deprived students who are too tired to learn, why not delay the school start by an hour or so? That is exactly what some enlightened physicians and educators are trying in Minnesota. In 1994, Dr. Barbara Yawn (no kidding), representing the Minnesota Medical Association, sent a letter to high schools in the state encouraging them to eliminate early school starts for teenagers.

The first school system to seriously explore the change was in Edina, a suburb of Minneapolis. They did a thorough study of as many of the ramifications of a later school start as they could imagine, and decided to implement the plan in September 1996. As of the writing of this book, there has been too little time for a complete analysis of the results of this change, but it appears to have been very positive—so positive that the late start time has been adopted by the other high schools in the Minneapolis area and a few other cities scattered around the country. Students like the later start time, and teachers feel that they are seeing more students who are "more engaged" in what they are doing ... "more focused." The changes in the schedules of athletic teams and extracurricular activities have been absorbed without major difficulties.

You can obtain an information packet from the Edina, Minnesota, school system that explains exactly how they were able to manage the transition to a later start time. Share it with your own school administrators. They may be eager to hear how another school district created a schedule that helped its students arrive in class more prepared to learn.

For Safety's Sake

Although a string of failing grades on your child's report card may be very upsetting, you must admit that D's and F's aren't life threatening. You may want to kill her when you see her grades, but your teenager isn't going to wake tomorrow morning in the intensive care unit because she came home today with an F on her geometry final. However, sleep deprivation can have serious and fatal consequences. At least one survey has determined that motor vehicle accidents are the second leading cause of death in the fifteen to twenty-four years age group. It has been estimated that each year 200,000 automobile accidents may be sleep re-lated. Long-haul truckers aren't the only drivers who fall asleep at the wheel. It can happen to any of us, even in broad daylight, if we are missing a few hours of sleep.

It is frightening to think what can happen when an inexperi-enced, sleep-deprived teenager climbs behind the wheel of a two-thousand-pound motor vehicle. Even without the addition of a little alcohol, we have the potential for a deadly mix. If your adolescent's poor grades haven't already forced you to take her sleep debt seriously, her safety should.

Is Your Teenager Sick or Tired . . .
or Depressed?

No matter what you do, your teenager will probably always be a little bit sleep-deprived. Even most of the high school students in Edina, Minnesota, will be tired when they arrive at school each morning, because the delayed school start can't completely com-pensate for their late bedtimes. Some of those adolescents will be so sleep-deprived that their behavior and ability to learn will be adversely effected. How will you know if your teenager is one of those having serious problems as the result of sleep deprivation?

Some adolescents make it easy by complaining that they feel tired all the time. In fact, if one eliminates sore throats and ath-letic injuries from the list, fatigue is the most common reason that parents bring their teenagers to my office. At least once or twice each week I am asked to examine an adolescent because her parents hope that I will find a treatable medical condition that might explain why their daughter always says she is tired. In almost every case my examination is unrevealing, and a simple mathematical calculation makes it clear that the teenager is simply not getting enough sleep.

Unfortunately, your teenager may not make the diagnosis of fatigue so obvious. She may not complain of being tired, and her behavior may not make you suspect sleep deprivation. Below is a list of some symptoms that sleep researchers have observed in their studies of sleep-deprived individuals:

- information–processing and memory deficits

- decreased ability to handle complex tasks

- decreased creativity

- hypersexuality

- irritability

- depression

- anxiety

School Problems

The first three items on the list above are obviously related to school success or failure and should remind you to question your adolescent's sleep patterns if she is having academic problems. This is particularly true if your child did not begin having trouble in school until she reached puberty.

Why does she say she is getting poor grades? What do the teachers say? Ask if she is feeling sleepy in school. Is there a pattern to the classes in which she is having the most trouble? Could she be struggling with the morning classes because she isn't fully awake until just before lunch? Or is she getting drowsy immediately after lunch? Is she trying to do her homework, but by the time she sits down to work she is too tired to do it efficiently?

Unfortunately, the answer may be that your child is just lazy or unmotivated. On the other hand, she may have a learning disability that did not appear until her schoolwork became more challenging. Ask her why she thinks she isn't performing up to expectations. Talk to the guidance counselors. Make sure that her academic talents and deficits have been thoroughly tested, and at the same time think about her sleep habits. How many hours is she sleeping at night? Remember, nine or more is the optimum. Is she hard to wake in the morning? How long does she sleep on the weekends? This may be a clue that she really needs more sleep and her body is trying to catch up on the weekends. It is unlikely that sleep deprivation is the only explanation for her school problems, and don't let your teenager use it as an excuse for every poor report card. However, always keep fatigue in mind as you investigate the other more traditional causes for her poor school performance.

Oh, That "Attitude"!

With puberty the pleasant and sunny disposition of childhood seems to vanish in a cloud of hormones. As a group, teenagers have earned a reputation for having rather difficult personalities. Although some of them can offer a cheerful face to the public, most parents must endure a darker side of their adolescent children. Irritability, moodiness, back talk, and rebelliousness in various forms seem to be par for the course for many teenagers.

I am sure that hormonal changes are at the heart of most of these unpleasant personality changes. However, you know as well as I do that we all get cranky when we get overtired. Teenagers are no different, and as they pass through puberty they will wake most mornings with a one- or two-hour sleep debt. No wonder adolescents have a reputation for being irascible.

I don't think there is a reliable test to determine whether your teenager has adopted an "attitude" because she is tired or because her internal workings are undergoing a major rearrangement. However, you should at least consider fatigue as a possibility when life with your adolescent seems to be just one confrontation after another. There might not be too much you can do about it, but the thought may make you feel better as you finish your third argument of the day.

Depression, Cause or Effect?

Teenage suicide seems to be reaching epidemic proportions in America. The suicide rate for ten-to-fourteen-year-olds has doubled since 1980, and it is not surprising that more and more parents are watching fearfully for signs of depression in their adolescents. You may already have begun to worry because your teenager is spending more time in her room and withdrawing from many of her friendships and activities. Someone may have warned you that your adolescent's complaints of being tired all the time could mean that she is depressed. To add confusion to your worry, look back at the list on page 187. Depression can be a symptom of sleep deprivation. Is your teenager tired because she is depressed or depressed because she isn't getting enough sleep? Or is it a combination? Obviously, I can't answer this question for you.

My advice to you would be the same advice I give to my patients here in Maine. If you are concerned that your child is depressed, because she is acting sad and withdrawn, and/or if she complains of being tired, begin by encouraging her to go to bed earlier and get some more sleep. If this doesn't help or things seem more serious, you should have her examined by her doctor to rule out a medical problem and then consult a psychologist or psychiatrist for an evaluation.

Tired and Sick

Although most teenagers are tired because they aren't getting enough sleep, occasionally illness can be the culprit. There are two medical conditions that deserve special mention. The first is *anemia*. As your child enters puberty her body begins to grow more rapidly. If her diet does not contain sufficient iron to keep up with this growth, she will become anemic. This problem is more likely to occur in young women because they begin to lose blood (and iron) with their menses.

One of the most common symptoms of anemia is fatigue, and you should make sure that your overtired teenager has a simple blood test to rule out the condition. The treatment consists of an iron supplement and some dietary advice.

Infectious mononucleosis is the other common disease that is likely to exhaust your adolescent. Mono is caused by a virus that can infect many different cells in her body, but it usually begins with a severe sore throat and swollen glands. This stage of the illness can last for up to two weeks, during which the unfortunate victim may be feverish and quite uncomfortable. Before the discomfort subsides fatigue becomes the most obvious and frustrating symptom. It may last for a few days but is more likely to persist for a month or two. Some victims never have much of a sore throat but nonetheless suffer from the fatigue. The old name of "the kissing disease" is a reminder to us that the virus is concentrated in saliva and so may be spread by kissing and sharing soft drinks, two behaviors you and I are powerless to prevent.

Although there are some controversial treatments for the initial sore throat, there is no remedy for the fatigue except rest. A few fortunate teenagers will have a mild case and never miss a day of school, but it is more likely that if your child catches mono she will miss several weeks of school. Most school systems are very familiar with the illness and will help you arrange for home tutors and a gradual return to classes as the fatigue subsides. Extracurricular activities and your child's social life will have to be curtailed until her strength returns. Many viral illnesses are followed by brief periods of fatigue, but none is as dramatic and frustrating as mono.

Chronic Fatigue Syndrome

There are thousands of teenagers and adults who feel exhausted despite getting what would seem to be adequate amounts of sleep. Initially, they may have been suspected as having mono or some other virus, but all of the tests have returned negative. The fatigue may persist for many months or years, far longer than one would expect from one of the common illnesses.

Some physicians have been tempted to group these unfortunate individuals together and label them as having *Chronic Fatigue Syndrome*. Support groups have been formed and research studies have been launched. To date there has been little progress in finding an explanation for the condition, and many physicians, including myself, doubt that a single cause will ever be discovered because none exists. I suspect that most of the teenagers who have been told they have Chronic Fatigue Syndrome actually have undiagnosed depression or may not have had a thorough investigation of their sleep habits.

Although I will stop short of saying that Chronic Fatigue Syndrome does not exist, I urge you to seek a second, and even a third, opinion before you accept a diagnosis of CFS for your child's symptoms. Include a psychiatrist and a sleep expert in your investigation. In more than twenty-five years of practice I can't recall seeing a single adolescent who has been successfully diagnosed with Chronic Fatigue Syndrome. There has always been another explanation or the patient has improved with more sleep.

> *Before accepting the diagnosis of Chronic Fatigue Syndrome, seek several opinions and consider including a psychiatrist or a sleep expert in your list of consultants.*

You Might Have Lucked Out and Found a Lark in Your Nest

Although a well-rested adolescent might be the exception, you may be lucky and have one of these strange birds in your nest. Rejoice! But don't get too smug. I am not sure that you or I can take much credit for your good fortune. I would like to claim that by raising a well-rested child you were guaranteed to have a well-rested teenager, but I am unaware of any research so far that supports this boast . . . though I keep hoping.

Some of us just seem to come into the world with the genetic material that enables us to get up early and function best in the morning. Sleep researchers call us "larks." We are "morning people," and if we go to bed early enough, research has shown, we will do better in school than "owls," the term used to describe "night people."

As you have learned, most teenagers are owls. With puberty they tend to go to bed and get up later, and there may not be a whole lot we can do about it. However, don't give up without a fight. The next section will provide you with a list of strategies to try. Some of them may work. If you have been blessed with a lark you should thank your lucky stars and skip on to the next chapter.

What Is a Parent to Do?

Parenting is sometimes described as a gradual process of letting go until your child is functioning independently as an adult. Adolescence should be the last stage in that process and is usually the most difficult. The dangers of alcohol, drugs, fast cars, and unprotected sex lurk around every corner. You want to keep a tight rein on your teenager to protect her, but the harder you try to maintain control the more she resists. Part of you knows that you must give her some freedom to make her own decisions, but the risks are frightening and very real. The following suggestions for helping keep your teenager stay better rested (*well* rested may be too much to hope for) are just that . . . suggestions. I understand that compliance may be difficult to obtain, but don't give up before you start. Give some of them a try.

Enforce an Early Bedtime

Remember that your teenager needs more than nine hours of sleep each night to be alert during the day. Move this issue up near the top of your priority list. Use whatever leverage you can wield to enforce a healthy bedtime. Make privileges such as phone and television time, approval to play sports, and the use of a motor vehicle contingent on a healthy into-bed-lights-out time. You have never been able to force your child to sleep, but you can do everything possible to create a situation in which there is little else for her to do but sleep. In other words, if you allow your teenager to stay up watching television until 11 on school nights, you are enabling her to become sleep-deprived by your failure to set healthy limits.

No TV in the Bedroom!

You read this admonition way back in Chapter 10. It is even better advice now that your child has reached puberty. A healthy and academically successful adolescent just won't have time to get her schoolwork accomplished, participate in extracurricular activities, get enough sleep, *and* watch more than an hour of TV on weekdays. Television has evil and magnetic powers and will encourage your child to stay awake well past her healthy bedtime. If you have provided her with a TV set in her bedroom, you are aiding one of your teenager's biggest enemies: fatigue.

Discourage Napping

When your child was a preschooler, I pleaded with you to do everything in your power to preserve her naps. Now that she is a teenager, naps can be your child's undoing. If you allow her to nap for more than ten or fifteen minutes in the afternoon, you run the risk of aggravating your adolescent's natural tendency to stay up late. Anything more than a short "power nap" may repay just enough of her sleep debt that she won't feel sleepy until midnight or later. If her school schedule allowed her to sleep until noon this might not be a problem. However, you and I know that even a Minnesota-style school start of 8:30 or 9 is going to mean that she will go off to class seriously sleep-deprived.

> *A nap of more than ten or fifteen minutes can aggravate your adolescent's natural tendency to stay up late.*

Some of us have learned how to refresh ourselves by lying down for ten or fifteen minutes and taking a "power nap." These are particularly helpful when we are tempted to succumb to the after-lunch drowsiness most of us encounter. Although short naps of less than half an hour may make us feel better and improve our productivity, they don't seem to do much to repay our sleep debt. The good news is that they won't interfere with our ability to fall asleep at night. However, if your teenager conks off for an hour or two in the afternoon that doesn't qualify as a "power nap," and she probably won't be sleepy at an appropriate bedtime.

Struggle to Keep Weekend Schedules Healthy

Protecting your teenager from school sleep lag may be your most difficult challenge. Remember that if on weekends your adolescent goes to bed even later and is allowed to sleep well past her usual schoolday wake-up time she will be more difficult to awaken during the week. She will arrive in school sleepy and statistically will do more poorly than her peers who are not suffering from sleep lag.

The solution may require you to create and enforce curfews and bedtimes that your teenager will view as cruel and unusual punishment. Obviously your child should be allowed to stay up a bit later on weekends, but midnight seems more than reasonable. On Saturday and Sunday mornings you should allow your adolescent to sleep an hour or two longer than her usual weekday time, because this will help her repay some of her debt. But permitting her to sleep longer enables her to incur a school sleep lag that will jeopardize her school success and probably aggravate her "attitude." If she complains that she is tired all the time and that you aren't allowing her to get enough sleep, point out that the solution is to go to bed earlier. This is particularly important on Sunday night.

It will make your job easier if you have created some reason for your teenager to wake up earlier on the weekends. Church attendance, projects around the house, and trips to visit family are just a few of the possibilities. I can hear many of you groaning that you will never be able to interest your adolescent in these activities. I agree that it may be difficult, but don't give up so easily. Move the issue to the front burner. You have more power than you think. You still control the money, the phone, and . . . the car keys.

Warn Her About Overcommitment

When your child was starting out in school I cautioned you about the perils of overcommitment to extracurricular activities and unrealistic schedules. Although you may not have realized it, you were in ultimate control of the situation then because you were the one who drove the minivan. However, your teenager can now probably sign up for as many activities as she wants to and can ride the school bus or get a lift with friends. You have been relegated to a position as an adviser. But even though she may not listen to your advice, help her calculate whether she is going to have enough time to play soccer, join the Future Teachers of America, volunteer for a shift at the soup kitchen, get her homework done, and get a healthy amount of sleep.

Ask her to speak to the guidance counselor at school or someone in a college admissions office. They should tell her that colleges are no longer impressed with how many activities the applicants have listed, but they are looking for what the student has accomplished. How deep was her involvement in an activity? In simplest terms, colleges are looking for quality, not quantity, when it comes to extracurricular activities.

If she ignores you and becomes overcommitted, bite your tongue and help her figure out a polite way of disentangling herself from some of her activities. It is tempting to say "I told you so," but we both know it serves no purpose. Just get on with the business of helping her restructure her schedule so she can get some much-needed sleep. She will thank you . . .later.

Don't Allow Her to Be Seduced by a Paycheck

Although you may rejoice that your teenager has discovered that having a job makes her feel important and provides her with money to spend, you must help protect her from the seductive power of a paycheck. Her employer's pleas for extra hours and the reward of more money for clothes or CDs may tempt your child to overcommit to her after-school job. She may or may not still find time for her homework, but the first sacrifice she is going to make is her sleep.

When she applies for a job help your teenager make a realistic estimate about what impact the job will have on her schedule, particularly her sleep. It is important to help your child understand that college is expensive and that she will be expected to contribute something toward the cost of her education. However, do not put so much emphasis on her responsibility that she feels compelled to work an unhealthy number of hours. Your adolescent needs some time to enjoy life, do her schoolwork, and . . . sleep. If money for college is a serious problem and loans and scholarships just aren't going to fill the gap, consider deferring matriculation for a year or two. That is a far better solution than watching your adolescent incur an unhealthy sleep debt while she is in high school.

Most states have child labor laws that should help you protect your teenager from the seductive employers, but these laws are often poorly enforced, and you may have to step forward and put your foot down. There are more important things than money, and sometimes sleep is one of them.

Encourage Healthy Study Habits

Although for the most part you are relegated to the role of adviser when it comes to your teenager's study habits, don't be afraid to point out that for most us an hour of study after nine or ten o'clock is less effective than an hour of study done earlier in the evening. I find that many of the highly motivated students in my practice, particularly young women, often spend too much time studying because they aren't doing it efficiently and are trying to study when they are exhausted. For these students, who may actually be larks, often the solution is to go to bed when they are feeling tired and get up a bit earlier the next morning to finish up when they are fresh.

Help your teenager realize when she is too tired to study efficiently. Point out that she actually may do better on a test by investing some of her study time in sleeping. Of course, you don't want this philosophy to become transformed into an excuse that will come back to haunt you: "Elaine, have you studied at all for your geometry test?" "No, Dad, I've decided to go to bed instead. You've always said sleep was more important."

Remember to keep tight control over the television and the Internet. Studies and sleep come first. These electronic addictions should be used as rewards at the end of studying.

Encourage Regular Exercise

If your teenager complains that she is having trouble falling asleep at night, part of the problem may be that she is not getting enough exercise. It is unclear exactly why regular exercise, particularly if it is done outside, helps sleep patterns. However, it probably has some role in establishing or reinforcing the circadian rhythms that influence our sleep-awake cycles.

Encourage your adolescent to participate in organized school sports, because they are an easy way to prevent couch potato inactivity. Unfortunately, some teams limit participation by "cutting" the less-talented participants, but do your best to guide your child toward sports that are open to all comers. I know some teams practice in the evening, and this arrangement can make it difficult for their members to wind down in time for a healthy bedtime. Do what you can to encourage the school to schedule practices earlier in the day. But if I had a choice, I would rather my child was physically active late in the day than not at all.

If your teenager is just not into sports, as many aren't, you must be both imaginative and persistent in finding ways to keep her physically active. One strategy is to post a list of household chores, preferably ones that need to be done outdoors and require at least half an hour of vigorous activity. Establish a house rule that one of these chores must be completed each day. Make television time, driving time, and phone time, among other things, contingent upon completion of this not-so-hard labor. If your adolescent can provide evidence that she has gotten some good exercise in some other form, you can allow this to replace a chore on occasion. Don't count physical education in school toward this requirement for activity. Unfortunately, most P.E. classes won't provide your child with enough exercise to help her sleep patterns.

Keep Control of Caffeine

If your teenager is having trouble getting to sleep or complains that she is waking at night and can't get back to sleep, inquire about her caffeine intake. If she is drinking caffeine-containing beverages in the afternoon and evening, do what you can to stop the practice. At a minimum just don't buy the stuff. If that means that other family members must do without, it is probably better for them to abstain as well.

Remember, You Still Hold the Keys

We are a society that has allowed itself to become dependent on the automobile. Getting a driver's license is a rite of passage whose importance cannot be underestimated. The ability to drive a car brings with it status and freedom, but remember that driving is a privilege and not a right guaranteed by law. You still hold the ultimate power over this privilege because you hold the keys. You own the car. Too few parents use this power to leverage against unhealthy and dangerous behavior. Your child's curfews, bedtimes, and other schedules are important for her own health and safety. Make them carefully and be reasonable. Remember, sleep is important—and don't forget that you hold the keys.

Summary of Strategies

- Encourage your school system to delay school start for high school students.

- Enforce an early bedtime.

- No TV in the bedroom.

- Discourage napping.

- Strive to keep your teenager's weekend sleep schedule as similar to her weekday schedule as possible.

- Discourage overcommitment to after-school work and activities.

- Encourage regular exercise.

- Discourage caffeine.

12

IT TAKES A WELL-RESTED PARENT TO RAISE A WELL-RESTED CHILD

Parenting Is Hard Work

To be good at parenting you must be well rested. In the first few months of life your baby will be up at night feeding frequently, and your usual sleep pattern is going to be interrupted. One sleep expert has calculated that by welcoming a new baby into your life you can expect to lose between 400 and 750 hours of sleep by the time he turns one. Your child is dependent upon you for many, if not all, of his physical needs. There is laundry to be done, cribs to be made up, spit-up to be cleaned up, diapers to be changed. All of these things take time and energy, and you will need to find time in your life and gas in your tank to get them done. If your only previous experience with this kind of responsibility has been taking care of a dog or a cat, you had better be prepared for a quantum jump in your energy expenditure.

The demands on your time and energy abate only slightly when your child moves into his second year of life. Feeding and diaper changing are replaced by carpooling and playgroups. As your child gets older you will continue to be his playmate, but you will begin to follow your child around to his out-of-the-home and after-school activities: soccer games, piano recitals—it goes on and on.

Your children will probably always be the leading cause of your lost sleep. When they are first born you will be up to feed them. When they are ill you will either be up tending to them or you will lie awake worrying if they will be okay until morning, when you will see the pediatrician. When they are teenagers you will be waiting for them to come home at night. Even when they are grown and out of the house you will lose sleep worrying about their future, their marriages, their jobs, and anything else that probably isn't any of your business.

> *Your children will probably always be the leading cause of your lost sleep.*

Are You Too Tired to Be Patient?

Parenting requires patience, a lot of patience, and you must be well rested to be a patient parent. The more fatigued you are the shorter your fuse will become. It makes us all uncomfortable to realize that we are all potential child abusers. You may not believe that you are capable of abusing your own child, but when you are functioning with only two hours of sleep and your child is screaming, your best intentions and upbringing can let you down. We are each equipped with differing amounts of patience when it comes to child-rearing, but we all have a breaking point.

There are many factors that can bring you closer to that point. Social isolation, lack of a family support structure, and ignorance about normal child development are known to predispose parents to child abuse, but fatigue is often the straw that breaks the camel's back. Occasionally a parent confides in me that he or she has struck a child in anger or is worried that he or she might abuse a child. Often that parent had become exhausted and in that irrational state had been unable to find a better alternative than physical force. We begin by finding out what factors have created the fatigue. When parents are no longer sleep-deprived they usually find it much easier to cope with their children's behavior. By keeping yourself well rested your fuse will be nice and long, and you will stay safely above the end of your rope.

Are You Too Tired to Be an Effective Parent?

Even the most well-behaved child requires some discipline from time to time. If you are going to be an effective parent, you must be able to set reasonable limits and then follow up with rational consequences if your child oversteps those limits. This is one of the most difficult jobs for any parent, and to do it well you must be well rested. You are more likely to get into screaming matches with your child and make threats that you can't follow up if you are tired. Your child is more likely to misbehave late in the day, when he is tired. If you have allowed yourself to finish your day exhausted, you aren't going to be in any shape to safely and effectively meet this discipline challenge.

Are You Too Tired to Parent Safely?

To be successful in this important job of parenting you must be well rested. You must be sharp and alert to protect your child from the dangers lurking in even the most childproofed home. Remember, you are going to be the lifeguard for your child, and you will never go off duty. We know that airline pilots and truck drivers are more likely to have accidents when they are exhausted. The safety of your child is no less important than a passenger on an airplane.

In my pediatric practice I have seen many children who accidentally poisoned themselves or sustained a serious injury while a parent had nodded off or because the parent was so fatigued that his or her powers of observation and judgment were impaired.

Hour after hour, day after day, you will be making hundreds of little and big decisions: "Is he playing too close to the road?" "Have I put away the furniture polish, and is the safety cap on tight?" "Can I wait until morning to call the doctor about his breathing?" You must be well rested to make the kind of choices that will make you a good parent and that will allow your child to grow up in a safe environment. Most "accidents" don't just happen. Many of them can be prevented by an alert parent.

Are You Too Tired to Be Cheerful?

How do you remember your parents? Were they upbeat and cheerful, or were they cranky and burned out? I am sure that you don't want to be remembered by your children as a grump. If you come home from work frazzled and exhausted, this is the way your child will recall you. Pace yourself, get your rest, and get to bed on time, so that whether you have been holding down the home front or working out in the job market, you will be able to finish the day in a positive and pleasant frame of mind. Don't wait for the weekends to recharge your batteries. It won't impress your children. They will remember you at your worst, the way they see you most of the week. Children don't have the kind of patience that can wait for the happy parent to magically appear on the weekend.

> **Don't wait for the weekends to catch up on your sleep.**

Parenting should be fun almost all of the time. If you're not having fun there may be something wrong with your child, but it is more likely that you need to make some changes in your parenting style. Many parents suffer silently, thinking that being a parent means sleepless nights, cranky children, and no time for themselves or their spouses. They can see the rewards that having a child has brought them, but they think there must be a big price to pay. They find themselves in a parental boot camp that must be endured to earn their stripes as a parent. Sadly, most of those parents are suffering needlessly. If they could learn a few simple strategies for getting their children and themselves some more sleep, they would realize how wonderful parenthood can be.

Depression is an unfortunately common problem for parents, mothers in particular. A recent study done at Dartmouth Medical School found that nearly half of the mothers of toddlers show signs of depression. "Baby Blues," or postpartum depression, is a well-known but infrequently discussed problem for mothers in the first six months after delivery. There are many factors involved in the development of depression, but scientists have discovered that fatigue and sleep deprivation are major contributors. By keeping yourself well rested you are more likely to meet the challenges of parenting without slipping under the cloud of depression.

Your Marriage and Your Spouse Deserve Some Quality Time

A successful marriage doesn't just happen; it requires care and feeding. It takes time. This means that your spouse deserves and needs some quality time, time not shared with anything or anyone else, not even your precious new child. Below you will find two bar graphs that depict how your day might change before and after children. Notice in the second graph that the quality spouse time or marriage renewal time has almost disappeared. Even the best marriage is going to have trouble surviving a situation like this for very long. I am sure some of the increase in the divorce rate in this country is due to fatigued, overworked parents who have not left enough time for their marriages. By the end of the day they are so burned out that they have little patience with their spouses and unfortunately say things they don't mean and that can't be easily undone.

Pre-Baby Schedule

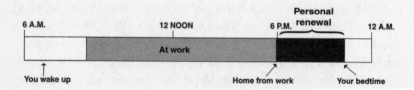

After-Baby Schedule

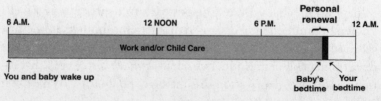

Each day you should strive to leave at least two hours (three would be even better) for your spouse and your marriage. Use this time for whatever you wish. It could be sexual intimacy, it could be talking, it could be playing Scrabble, it could be just spending silent time together reading, knitting . . . just being together. Your bar graph should look like this third graph. With the help of this book your life can approximate the proportions depicted in this graph.

A Better After-Baby Schedule

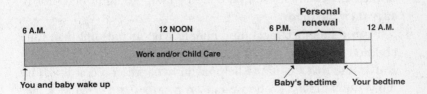

It is a mistake to postpone this "together time" until the weekend—or even worse, until sometime next month. This is not to say that I frown on parents taking a weekend away together every now and then, but I have observed that most marriages need renewal on a daily basis. Marriage is like a houseplant that needs watering on a frequent schedule; it is not like a cactus that can be watered once every several months.

> *Budget enough time and energy for yourself and your marriage.*

Remember that you are building a family. Unfortunately, many parents attempt to employ a child-centered parenting style. By focusing all of their energy on their child, they shortchange themselves and their spouses. A family is a collection of compromises. The trick is to make the right compromises so that each member can thrive as an individual. Budget enough time and energy for yourself and your marriage. You not only deserve it, you need it!

Parents Need a Good Bedtime, Too

All of this means that you should strive to have a nice early bedtime for yourselves *and* your child. If you are going to be a patient, cheerful, and safe parent you need to be well rested, and this of course means a decent bedtime. Many parents manage to get to bed early enough themselves but because they haven't been able to get their children to bed at a reasonable hour, they have not left any time for each other and end up going to bed shortly after their children.

I can remember meeting a couple who at the time had four children under the age of six. Both parents appeared so healthy and at ease that I couldn't help asking what their secret was. The reply was simple. The house ran on routines and schedules that were not overly rigid but included family meals, outside playtime, and children's bedtimes of about 7. The parents had the next two or three hours to themselves. Prompted by this meeting I began to question other parents who seemed to be more contented than average. Almost uniformly I found that their children had bedtimes early enough to assure that the parents could have a couple of hours of quality together time and still get a good night's sleep.

Sometimes the problem stems from work schedules that do not allow for family or spousal time. Finding time for your family, yourself, your job, *and* getting enough sleep can be difficult. It may take a while to achieve, but it is a goal that deserves your top priority. Be creative and assertive when it comes to your work schedules. Explore job sharing, flexible schedules, and other negotiated arrangements that allow for together time and a decent bedtime that will leave you both as rested parents and spouses.

If you are able to get to bed at a decent hour but have trouble sleeping once you lie down, I recommend two books you might find helpful. They are *Power Sleep,* by Dr. James B. Maas, and *Sleep*

Thieves, by Stanley Coren. Both authors suggest strategies for improving your sleep. As a place to start, get some regular exercise and fresh air, avoid alcohol and caffeine, and try to maintain a consistent bedtime routine. It is very likely that once your child begins to get enough sleep and rest your sleep problems will improve dramatically.

Summary of Strategies

- Establish a healthy bedtime for yourself.

- Create a bedtime for your child that gives you two hours of time for yourself and your marriage.

- Don't wait for the weekend to catch up on your sleep.

- Give your family's sleep requirements a high priority when you are planning work and commuting schedules.

13

Your Last Chance

You have given it your best shot. You courageously moved her into her own bedroom before she was a week old. You resisted the temptation to share your bed with her during the those first trying weeks. It was difficult to listen to her cry, but by the time she was a month old, you had helped her learn to put herself to sleep in her own crib. By reprioritizing your life you were able to provide your child with a healthy bedtime that allowed you and your spouse to have time for yourselves and for each other.

By carefully choosing a day care that was sleep-friendly and by keeping your schedule lean, you were able to encourage your toddler to keep both of her naps until she was nearly two. You were rewarded with a child whose behavior was the envy of your friends and family. When it was time to give up one of the naps, you welded the remaining one to lunch and created a siesta that kept her well rested through her remaining preschool years.

When she finally entered school and was exposed to the cornucopia of activities your community could offer, you were able to help her resist the temptation to join every team and sign up for every club that was available. You became skilled at operating your VCR and managed to preserve an early bedtime when her peers were showing up at school each morning in a sleep-deprived state.

Adolescence was your biggest challenge, but you tried to help your teenager find the time to catch up on the sleep that was being lost to her school and social calendars. When you could, you leveraged driving privileges against reasonable bedtimes, but it was getting more difficult because the time to let go was approaching.

With or without this book you have done a masterful job of raising a well-rested child. However, it is time for your little bird to leave the nest. High school graduation is just around the corner, and then it is off to college, or into the navy, or to her own apartment downtown. Will she be able to stay well rested without your help?

College ... Do you remember what it was like? Noisy dorms. Roommates that stayed up all night playing cards or studying (or both) and then slept through classes the next day. Parties on the weekends and at least one weekday night. Getting enough sleep at night is not a high priority for most college students. Early-morning classes are traditionally underfilled and seldom attended by those few who have been foolish enough to sign up. Although unwilling to admit that they are still adolescents, these young adults often have the same sleep needs they did when they were in high school. In a study of Brown University students, scientists discovered that college students were going to bed and getting up three hours later than they did in high school.

It is a frightening vision. You have worked so hard to raise your child in an atmosphere that preserved and treasured her need for sleep, and now you are going to throw her to the wolves. How will she survive in an environment where sleep deprivation is the norm? I don't know, and I must admit that I worry along with you. The psychosocial pressures that exist in college create such an abrupt change in sleep habits that it is difficult for any eighteen-year-old to adapt. As one sleep specialist (Mary Carskadon) has observed, "Until sleep gets more respect, it's swimming upstream to try to maintain good sleep habits in college." (*JAMA,* Sept. 18, 1996).

It really is out of our hands. Although you and I are reaching deep into our pockets to help foot the bill, we are sending our grown children out to become young adults and we must let them make their own decisions. However, if your child has become accustomed to being well rested, you should at least make a few suggestions as she fills out her college housing applications. Remind her how she feels and acts and functions when she is tired. Encourage her to sign up for the "quiet dorm" or at least opt for a single room. If she must have a roommate, suggest that she request someone who also values her sleep and tends to go to bed early.

Of course, all of this good advice may go in one ear and out the other, but who knows? Your efforts at emphasizing fatigue prevention for the last eighteen years may have rubbed off, and your child/adult may make the right choices. On the other hand, she may not, but by Thanksgiving she may have realized that he isn't going to survive her freshman year unless she finds a single room or a less-raucous dorm. You can mutter "I told you so" under your breath if you wish, but make one last effort for your not-so-rested child. Encourage her to call the appropriate office to make a housing change, or even make the call for her if she is hesitant.

If your child has joined the military and your baby is in the hands of drill sergeants, you can hope that a schedule that begins with reveille in the morning and lights-out at night will help preserve some of the sleep habits you introduced, at least for a while. However, if your child is striking out on her own with a job and an apartment, you can only hope for the best. She probably will be staying up too late partying or watching TV. Don't get discouraged; you have done your job. You have raised a well-rested child, and I bet that in the long run she will remember that getting enough sleep was an important part of her childhood. However, just in case she doesn't, save this book on your shelf and give it to her as a baby shower gift.

14

No One Ever Promised You It Was Going to Be Easy

Here in Brunswick, Maine, I may be known as the doctor who tells all of the parents in his practice to put their children to bed earlier, but I hope that after reading *Is My Child Overtired?* you understand that there is much more to successful parenting than merely enforcing an early bedtime for your child.

Although for some fortunate parents the simple act of tucking their six-year-old in at 7:30 instead of 9 may eliminate the majority of their child's behavior problems, most parents, including yourself, will probably not be so lucky. For you the sleep solution might involve making numerous changes in your routine. An earlier bedtime may necessitate an earlier dinner, which means an earlier nap and consequently an earlier lunch. A more effective and efficient bedtime ritual may mean eliminating the rough-housing and physical play that you have come to enjoy after dinner. It may even mean that one of you won't be there for bedtime some evenings because your work schedule gets you home too late. These are not easy pills to swallow.

If you are a new parent, the sleep solution can help you raise a well-rested child from the very beginning, but you must be willing to accept the notion that your child can, and should, learn sleep independence. The process may not come as quickly as you would like, and it may require that you listen to your child cry, one of the most difficult things any parent can be asked to endure.

Children thrive on routine, but healthy routines often don't develop without some parental intervention. The sleep solution may require that you juggle your schedule while making some difficult choices about when and how you do things, simply to preserve your child's afternoon nap or maintain a healthy bedtime. By the time he has entered first grade, these choices may include saying no to some of his favorite extracurricular activities, because your child has become hurried and overcommitted to the point of exhaustion. When he reaches high school the decisions will be even more difficult because they can impact on such flash points as after-school employment, curfews, and driving privileges.

Although most parents can make relatively minor adjustments in their schedules and parenting styles to achieve the sleep solution, occasionally big problems demand big changes. Your work schedule or commuting arrangement simply may not leave enough hours in the day to allow you to raise a well-rested child. Major changes such as finding a new job or moving to a different neighborhood, closer to your work, may be required to achieve the sleep solution. Making these kinds of decisions is a far cry from doing a little tinkering with your child's bedtime.

Raising children should be fun, but I hope no one has promised you it will be easy. The sleep solution is a collection of strategies for successful parenting from birth to adolescence that are tied together by one common thread: the fact that providing your child and yourself adequate rest and sleep is essential for his health, his happiness, and ultimately his success as an adult. Unfortunately, it isn't always as simple as putting him to bed early.

I have tried to make the process seem less overwhelming by dividing it into smaller steps that you can build on as your child gets older. But even if you take little bites, there will be days when you will feel that you have bitten off more than you can chew. Stick with it and return to this book for help when parenting is more of a drag than a joy. I suspect you will find the solution somewhere in its pages.

INDEX

Index

bassinets, 47
bathing, in bedtime ritual, 70
bed buzzers, 123
bedrooms:
    baby without, 26–27
    shared by siblings, 154–55
    television in, 171, 193
beds:
    transition from crib to, 14,
      92–95
    weekend visitation and, 149–50
bed sharing, 24–25, 26, 44
    after-lunch siesta and, 105–6
    early risers and, 147
    nightmares and, 128
    night wakings and, 144
    sick child and, 137
    traveling and, 88, 89
bedtime, 11, 14, 68–69, 167, 211
    for adults, 148, 206–7
    for baby, 42–43
    with custodial vs. noncustodial
      parent, 150, 151
    early risers and, 147
    guidelines for, 68
    of older sibling, maintaining af-
      ter new baby's arrival,
      156–57
    sleep refusal and, 140
    slumber parties or sleepovers
      and, 178–79
    snacks at, 70–71
    of teenagers, 68, 182–83,
      184–85, 186, 193, 194–95
    television watching and, 171
bedtime rituals, 66–72, 211
    for adults, 67, 207
    changes in, as child ages, 66, 72
    elements of, 70–72
    participants in, 69–70
    for sibling of new baby, 156
    sleep refusal and, 140–43
    timing of, 68–69
bedwetting, 13, 122–23
    school schedule and, 163–64

weekend visitation and, 150
behavior problems, 12, 108–9, 202
bellyaches, 13, 121–22
biologic variation, 9, 116
biorhythms, 170, 182, 184, 198
blankets, attachment to, 47
    see also security objects
brain waves, 176
breakfast, 147–48
breastfeeding, 157
    baby's weight gain and, 33–34
    bed sharing and, 24, 25, 26
    feeding schedule and, 34
    length of feedings and, 39
    maternity leave and, 31
    pacifiers and, 50–51
    positive parental interaction
      during, 41
    at unpredictable times, 76
breathing problems, nocturnal,
    131–33, 169
burping, 47–48, 65

caffeine, 183, 198, 207
car rides:
    falling asleep during, 20
    "floating lunch" strategy and,
      103
    security objects and, 74–75, 86
cars:
    accidents and, 13, 186
    teenagers' privileges and, 199
car seats, 45
Carskadon, Mary, 209
cheerfulness, of parents, 203–4
child abuse, 13, 201
chronic fatigue syndrome (CFS),
    191
closets, converting into sleeping
    quarters for baby, 26
colds, 136–37
    ear infections and, 134
    snoring and, 132, 133
"cold-turkey" approach, 59, 60–61
    early risers and, 146

Index

Avoid mealtime battles while establishing healthful eating habits!

A Guide for the Perplexed Parent

Coping with a **Picky Eater**

William G. Wilkoff, M.D.

Coping with a Picky Eater • 0-684-83772-2 • $11.00 • Fireside